Spike Milligan (1918–2002) was one of the greatest and most influential comedians of the twentieth century. Over the course of his astonishing career he wrote over eighty books of fiction, memoir, poetry, plays, cartoons and children's stories.

Norma Farnes was Spike Milligan's agent, manager, mother confessor and friend for thirty-six years. Her books include *Spike: An Intimate Memoir*, *Memories of Milligan* and *Milligan's Meaning of Life*. She lives with her partner in London and Yorkshire.

Spike Milligan:
Man of Letters

Edited by Norma Farnes

PENGUIN BOOKS

PENGUIN BOOKS

Published by the Penguin Group
Penguin Books Ltd, 80 Strand, London WC2R ORL, England
Penguin Group (USA) Inc., 375 Hudson Street, New York, New York 10014, USA
Penguin Group (Canada), 90 Eglinton Avenue East, Suite 700, Toronto, Ontario, Canada M4P 2Y3
(a division of Pearson Penguin Canada Inc.)
Penguin Ireland, 25 St Stephen's Green, Dublin 2, Ireland (a division of Penguin Books Ltd)
Penguin Group (Australia), 707 Collins Street, Melbourne, Victoria 3008, Australia
(a division of Pearson Australia Group Pty Ltd)
Penguin Books India Pvt Ltd, 11 Community Centre, Panchsheel Park, New Delhi – 110 017, India
Penguin Group (NZ), 67 Apollo Drive, Rosedale, Auckland 0632, New Zealand
(a division of Pearson New Zealand Ltd)
Penguin Books (South Africa) (Pty) Ltd, Block D, Rosebank Office Park,
181 Jan Smuts Avenue, Parktown North, Gauteng 2193, South Africa

Penguin Books Ltd, Registered Offices: 80 Strand, London WC2R ORL, England

www.penguin.com

First published by Viking 2013
Published in Penguin Books 2014
001

Printed in Great Britain by Clays Ltd, St Ives plc

ISBN: 978-0-241-96692-1

www.greenpenguin.co.uk

MIX
Paper from
responsible sources
FSC www.fsc.org   FSC™ C018179

Penguin Books is committed to a sustainable
future for our business, our readers and our planet.
This book is made from Forest Stewardship
Council™ certified paper.

I would like to dedicate this book to the
Saint and Saintess
aka
Ashley and Gordon Blakeway
For everything.

Contents

Acknowledgements

I would like to thank:

All of the contributors to this book who gave their permission to publish their letters.

Will Hammond – my editor. It's such a pleasure to work with him (mind you, he thinks he's always right).

Christine Chism – for all her support.

Stuart and Nicola Knight – who prevented me from being homeless while compiling this tome.

'Kitchen' Ken Lane – for going that extra mile for me.

Aimee Charlton and Amanda Murray – for all the joy they give me.

Philip Hughes – for all his encouragement.

Jack Clarke – my old man, who is still putting up with me after thirty-six years. His medal is in the post.

Introduction

'Norma, my name is Will Hammond. I'm an editor at Viking Publishing.'

Me: 'Y-e-e-e-s?' Wondering what he wanted from me.

'I've been looking through our back catalogue and I'd like to talk to you about your books – *The Spike Milligan Letters*, Volumes One and Two.'

I knew he would want something. They always do.

We talked for a while and then I told him that in 1994 I had started to collate Volume Three and was possibly two-thirds of the way through that volume. I had not looked at it since that time because a million other things had taken over called life, and as Eric Sykes would say, 'It got put on the back burner.'

Will Hammond became full of enthusiasm and wanted to meet me. At the time I was frantically busy so we arranged a meeting three weeks hence. Mind you, he didn't tell me how charming he was and how devastatingly good-looking he is, or I would have cancelled everything and arranged to meet him the next day. What a pity he's not ten years younger!!!

Back to *The Spike Milligan Letters*. Volume One came about because I was going through a sticky patch and Spike wanted to help me. Remember he was once a flypaper (his, not mine).

This is an extract from my introduction to the first volume and I think it explains everything: 'I was going through a pretty bad patch – a divorce – Spike had been through it all, and knew the mental strain only too well. When he discovered I had to pay out money to stay in the flat I was living in – he was horrified. And, one morning, when all this was going on, he came into my office and said, "How are you off for bread? – badly, I'll bet – well I'll have to think of a way you can earn some extra," and walked out of the office.

'I had a lot on my mind at the time, and completely forgot all about it. Until about three or four days later, Spike came into my office and said, "I've been thinking about your bread situation," and I said, "Don't bother, I'll get a night job," and he said, "seriously, Norm, why don't you go through my files and collate some of my letters – ask the publisher if he is interested in putting them into a book. They might sell, and at least they will tide you over for a bit."

'And that's how it all started. Mind you, there was a condition. He didn't want to know anything about it, didn't want to be asked an opinion, didn't want to see the choice of letters, or be asked any questions at all (which you can imagine was difficult, making my own choice from thousands of letters he writes every year, to all and sundry). And the position it put me in. A truly magnanimous gesture on his part, and what if he didn't approve, because he still hasn't a clue of what is going into the book – what a position to be in? All he has ever said is, "Surprise me, and give me the first copy when it's ready." '

So when I bought a new car in 1994, Spike said to Eric, 'She's committed financial suicide again, she's bought herself a new car and I've told her she had better start on Volume Three, I thought I'd better warn you.'

So here it is. A handful of the letters in the following pages appeared in those two previous volumes. The rest have never been reproduced before.

I'm sitting at my desk flicking through Volume One and I'm smiling at some of the letters and notes. How did we live through all that drama and, more importantly, how did we survive?

After what seems like a thousand years, it's amazing that I can still smile at some of what I call Spike's 'Golden Moments'. To me some of them are worth repeating and I'd like to include a few notes alongside the letters. I'll mark them and I hope they may make you smile – if they make you laugh it's a bonus.

It's eleven years since Spike died (26 February 2002) and people still ask me, 'Do you miss him?'

Reading through the letters and notes in this book, how could I not? Of course I miss the old sod.

Norma Farnes
16 April 2013*

* Happy birthday, Spike.

Foreword

I've always wished to be a man of letters. Well apparently this book does it for me. Unbeknown to me my manager, under my very nose (in a crouching position) has all these years been secretly compiling a book from my correspondence. I often wondered what she was doing in my office. She never did a stroke of work for me. All the time *I* have been working for *her*. Time and time again she would come into my office when I was concentrating on a TV show, or a book and she would say 'You must rest, relax, why not write a letter to The Times or someone?', anything to stop me working. I would do her bidding. On the basis of this she is about to become rich. However I forgive her, and I will be back in the office next Monday morning working for her as usual.

Spike Milligan

[Spike's original foreword to the first volume of his letters, published in 1977.]

PART ONE
A Man of Letters

1

Assorted Misunderstandings

R. B. Hodges Esq.
The Director
Lyons/Tetley Limited
Greenford
Middlesex

4 April 1990

Dear Mr Hodges,

I can't imagine why you changed square tea bags to round ones because despite this change the tea still tastes the same, is it supposed to. Perhaps if you try an oblong one.

Sincerely,
Spike Milligan

———◆———

Lyons Tetley Limited
Greenford
Middlesex

3 May 1990

Dear Spike,

Many thanks for your letter and interest in our product.

Five years ago we started to develop our Round Tetley Teabag in secret. It all began with a belief that the shape would really appeal to consumers. Since the launch last year 1 million new buyers have confirmed that our instincts were right. People really do prefer the new round bags and many of them also feel they make a better brew.

You've certainly set us thinking about the oblong, although we feel at the moment our consumers are unlikely to find that as appealing as a round Tetley Teabag.

Thank you once again for writing and I hope you enjoy the selection of Lyons Tetley products which are enclosed with my compliments.

With best wishes.

Yours sincerely,
Ken Pringle
Marketing Director

―――――――◆―――――――

Ken Pringle Esq.
Marketing Director
Lyons Tetley Limited
Greenford
Middlesex

23 May 1990

Dear Ken,

Can you tell me when you changed from square to round, what did you do with the corners.

Sincerely,
Spike Milligan

―――――――◆―――――――

Lyons Tetley Limited
Greenford
Middlesex

12 June 1990

Dear Spike,

Thank you for your continued interest in our round Tetley teabags.

To produce these is not simply a case of cutting the corners off our old square bags. The process is slightly more complex than that, but any excess material that does result is carefully disposed of.

Yours sincerely,
K. Pringle
Marketing Director

(S) No bloody sense of humour at all he's missed the point. (N)

Ian Anthony Esq.
British Broadcasting Corporation

1 April 1982

Dear Ian,

Thank you for making a glorious cock-up of the timings between Australia and England, which resulted in phoning my brother whilst he was asleep, and possibly the worst fucking interview I have ever had in my life.

We must do it again sometime.

Sincerely,
Spike Milligan

[Ian Anthony replied: 'I don't know which of the bastards I work with gave you my name, but I had nothing to do with arranging your interview', and he suggested they had dinner.]

———•———

Ian Anthony Esq.

20 April 1982

Dear Ian,

Mea Culpa. So, the cock up about the cock ups are still going on.

Yes, I would love you to take me to dinner, and you can tell me (a) who you are, (b) how dare you have a sense of humour and work for a crowd of creeps like the BBC, and (c) I can tell you why I have a sense of humour and work for a crowd of creeps like the BBC, and (d) I can possibly glean some stories for my final book 'Aunty' which is now reaching massive proportions and should demolish the whole of the BBC on the first day of publication.

Love, light and peace,
Spike Milligan

———•———

The Editor
Daily Mail

22 May 1973

Dear Sir,

Your front page story May 22 suggested Peter Sellers and Liza
Minnelli are having an affair. This is an outrageous lie.
Peter and I have been secretly engaged for twelve years and
we are to be married in the spring as soon after the operation
as possible.

Sincerely,
Spike Milligan

HRH The Prince of Wales KGKT
Buckingham Palace

11 October 1988

Dear Prince Charles,

Serious for once. I have been commissioned by *The Mail on
Sunday* to write an article on you. Of course I have ensured it
is fair and just and no media hype. And to obey with courtesy,
I sent a copy of the article to your Press Secretary, Philip McKie.
(My God what a lunatic! Where did you get him from?) I mean,
never mind shooting stags in the Highlands, you should have
shot him. Anyhow I heard this lunatic 'has gone' and the silly
sod has mislaid the article I sent him to get your clearance.
So I got my Manager to telephone the Palace and she has spoken
to Dicky Arbiter and he is trying to locate Philip McKie to let
you see the article.

I just thought I would let you know that it's your end that has cocked it up.

CHARLES HAS COCKED IT UP AGAIN SAYS ARCH
GOON SPIKE MILLIGAN. DRUNKEN SCOTTISH
McGONAGALL-TYPE PRESS SECRETARY
ABSCONDS WITH INCRIMINATING DOCUMENTS
AND A ROLE OF INTIMATE FILM SHOWING
PRINCE CHARLES' UNUSED TOILET PAPER!

It is still the best country.

Love, light and peace,
Spike Milligan

9 Orme Court
LONDON W2

13 July 1978

Mr K Lyne
Supervisor
Zones 4 and 6
British Leyland
Services and Parts Division
Cowley
OXFORD

Dear Mr Lyne

I wonder if you can help me. I have a Mini GTX with
a Stage II engine. It does about 98 miles an hour
top speed. Is there an adaptation that will make it
do over 100 miles a hour? If so, could you give me
the information.
Could I have a reply before the Mini becomes extinct?
I say this because previous letters to British Leyland
have never got a reply.

Sincerely

Spike Milligan

SPIKE
This is THE VERY
REASON NO ONE WILL
GET IN THE CAR WITH YOU.

The Rt. Hon. Barbara Castle MP
Minister of Transport
c/o The House of Commons
London SW1

15 March 1968

Dear Barbara Castle,

Recently I lost my licence, having passed the Breathysler Test with flying colours.

In the case for the Prosecution, they said I was not drunk, but my alcohol content was above the lawful one.

Losing a licence for an ordinary 9a.m. to 5p.m. man in the street is not that difficult to live with, but in my case where I am moving from place to place non stop, it's becoming very very difficult, and expensive for me.

An ordinary day, a hire car picks me up at Finchley and takes me to my office £2. 0s. 0d. Taxi from office to rehearsal rooms 6/-d. As the rehearsal rooms are in an area miles away from taxis, I have to get a mini cab on the phone, as there is no phone in the building in which I am rehearsing, I have to go out and phone to take a car to take me back to the office 8/-d. Another private car to take me home at night, another £2. 0s. 0d. which is nearly £5. 0s. 0d. per day on cars. Then from home a car to the BBC to do a Late Night Show, and likewise a car back.

You can see the sort of day this is. This is having a great strain upon me, what with cars not turning up on time, and in this light it's affecting my work and my pocket alike.

Is there no way you can see fit, and I am speaking as a very law abiding citizen, who is not stupid enough to consume any alcohol in future before driving, if I could apply for the licence back earlier.

If I could come and talk to you, or meet you. I am not an irresponsible person, trying to get my licence back because I am too lazy to take the tube (it's a place I cannot travel on without getting clobbered for autographs).

Respectfully,
Spike Milligan

———◆———

Viscount Brentford
Automobile Association
London WC2

7 January 1972

Dear Sir,

Recently I arrived at my office to find that my car had had all four tyres let down by some joker.

I am a member of the AA, so I phoned them and a man came and charged me £1.85 for pumping up the tyres. This does not make me too happy as I am a member of the AA and I would like to know what are the circumstances which oblige me to pay a fee, when, in fact, the car was at my office and not outside my home, which makes it like a breakdown on any highway.

I would like to know, was I supposed to pay.

Respectfully,
Spike Milligan

———◆———

The Metropolitan Police
Central Ticket Office
London W1

23 May 1973

Dear Sirs,

I have today received a Parking Fine to be paid for my car.
It states on 28.02.73 Frith Street W.1. Car Registration No. is
HYT 927K.

On 27th February my car was stolen and I reported this to the
Police at Harrow Road, W2. The Police informed me that it had
not been towed away as they had checked and I had to report it
as stolen. On 28th February I was informed by the Harrow Road
Police that my car had been found in Frith Street and I had to go
to a pound near Kings Cross and I would be able to collect it. In
fact, on this particular day I was recording a show and my
Manager, Miss Norma Farnes went along to the pound near
Kings Cross, I believe it was Panton Street, NW1 and collected
the car. She was told that there would be nothing to pay as the
car had been stolen and when the car was collected there was a
parking fine on the car but I did not pay it because of the
circumstances.

Perhaps you would be good enough to let me know, due to
the circumstances that the car was stolen, whether in fact I have
to pay this fine No. 04 418 651 89 3. I look forward to hearing
from you.

Sincerely,
Spike Milligan   *S Keep trying Darling. N*

The Chief Clerk
Marylebone Magistrates Court
London W1

3 July 1973

Dear Sir,

On 29th June 1973 I went for an early morning swim at the Serpentine, Hyde Park. I returned after twenty minutes to find my car, which had been parked in the space provided next to Fortes Restaurant, with a parking fine on it. Now then, this car park is (a) off the main road, (b) there are no yellow lines, (c) there are no parking meters, (d) there was room for me to park along with the other cars parked there which I did. I discovered that there are small notices on the outskirts of this car park which are not easily discernible when parking in the car park which say, 'no parking allowed before 11 o'clock'. Tell me, what is the point of having an empty car park before 11.00 a.m.? To set up a car park to keep cars out until after 11.00 a.m. is asinine, to have an empty car park in a choked city is to increase the congestion, an empty space where a car should be parked is contrary to organization and common sense, in other words what is the point of having an empty car park?

Again, if they had a large notice at the entrance of the car park which you could not miss when you went in, saying 'no parking until after 11.00 a.m.' this would also help the situation.

As I say, it is outrageous, therefore I have no intention of paying the fine, I will not be in Court on the day requested and I shall not pay any extra fine as the result of my non-appearance, therefore your only way out is to send me to prison. I will gladly do this and make use of the media television and newspapers to put my point of view.

Respectfully,   *I said I won't pay*
Spike Milligan

William Davis Esq.
Punch Magazine

8 October 1974

Dear Bill,

I am sending you another photograph. The one you
keep publishing makes me feel I am suffering from a
severed head.

Love, light and peace,
Spike Milligan

———•———

The Chief Constable
Greater Manchester Police

14 November 1974

Dear Sir,
              Police Car Pound – Rochdale Road.
                      Manchester

This is to let you know that on the second time my car was towed
away, in two days, somebody at the Rochdale Car Pound took
the contents of my car and put them into a plastic bag.

    Among the contents was a tin of lubricating oil, which was
opened at the top, the result was everything was covered with oil,
it was the last straw for me in Manchester.

    Thank you very much for ruining my A A book, my Street
Map Guide to London and my first aid kit. If I never come to
Manchester again, it will be two weeks too soon for me.

Respectfully,
Spike Milligan
Dictated by Spike Milligan and signed in his absence

———•———

Greater Manchester Police
Chief Constable's Office

19 November 1974

Dear Mr Milligan,

Spike Milligan Motors (Incarcerated)

I was sorry to learn from your letter of 14th November, 1974 that you had the misfortune to have your car impounded twice in one day on your recent visit to Manchester.

The removal of the vehicle is one (or should it be two?) thing but it is clear that we did not look after your other property at the pound as well as we might. I hope you will accept the contents of this parcel in the friendly spirit in which it is sent.

The AA book and the London Street Guide are the latest editions, so maybe you have gained a bit of ground there.

While I hope that your relations with the police have not come to breaking point or that your feelings are not unduly wounded, it is obvious from your letter that they have been strained, so you might find something to soothe the situation in the First Aid Kit.

The latest increases in the price of oil (and the cost of posting a large can) rule out me sending anything more substantial than this small tin of three in one oil. As you can see from the diagram on the can it has multifarious uses, including the lubrication of bicycles, which might come in handy if you have the bad luck to lose your car again. The oil is also good for improving the performance of some crime prevention devices as well!

As the many admirers of your talents in Greater Manchester (among whom I number myself) would never forgive the police if you were put off returning to Manchester by your experiences, I am enclosing a clutch of straws as you lost your last one on the 6th – the corn is a bonus!

The Guide to Manchester shows the parking regulations and car parks and we all hope that should you soon come back to the North West, you will be able to avoid your car coming into our dragnet.

Yours sincerely,
R. S. Barratt
Deputy Chief Constable

R. S. Barratt Esq.
Deputy Chief Constable
Chief Constable's Office
Manchester

27 November 1974

Dear Lads,

Ta; all is forgiven.

I am now in the process of inventing an edible car. It would delight me to see a traffic warden approaching, and his astonished look as I gradually finished off the fenders, and bumpers, and with a dash of mustard, the steering wheel. I could then say the car was just passing through.

Love, light and peace,
Spike Milligan
Dictated by Spike Milligan and signed in his absence

---

9 METER BAY IN CAROLINE
PLACE EMPTY

ALL Meters
Booked. Residents
baup full –
I can't eat the
car
                Sprk Milligan

Parliamentary Under Secretary of State for Transport
Peter Bottomley MP
Department of Transport
London SW1

9 August 1988

Dear Mr Bottomley,

We don't seem to have gotten anywhere with my idea for a drink and drive commercial whereas in the process I am afraid I have got into trouble. You see, I am possibly a busier man than you and I phoned the number given to me which is your direct line. A lady answered and instead of saying 'Yes you can speak to him' – 'No you cannot speak to him', there was a MI5 atmosphere in which she said 'Who's speaking.' I said my name was Milligan. She did not seem to grasp it and after repeating it three times I spelled it for her.

The next question was 'What is the nature of your enquiry?' I explained at long length the nature of my call and was then told you were on holiday. I then said 'After spending five minutes answering your questions you now tell me he isn't fucking well there!'

I am sorry I exploded but I think it is imbecilic to ask a series of questions about things she can do nothing about and then to have been told the person I wanted to speak to is on holiday. Surely it would have been more intelligent to have told me that first. Anyway will you please tell her I am sorry.

I will try again. My God, why am I doing this? I make much more money writing books. I think it is called being a public-spirited citizen. If you have a telephone number – a more direct line where I will not be interrogated – I will be very grateful to have it.

Thank you very much,
Spike Milligan

Stewart K. Riddick and Partners
Chartered architect & surveyors
London N12

21 July 1981

Dear Mr Milligan

Re 930 High Road
Following our telephone conversation today, I wish to express my concern over your comment that you intend, if necessary, to break and enter the above premises – albeit you have confirmed the suggestion was made in jest. To avoid any further embarrassment I would like to place on record that should any information concerning the internal fabric of this building be obtained by yourselves or any third party, without my consent, then appropriate action will follow.

I would re-emphasize that I have given my word that once we resolve the planning situation with regard to the building I would be willing to allow you to have access to the interior before any demolition takes place.

Yours sincerely,
Stewart K. Riddick

[This building was being demolished. Spike wanted to retrieve a memento for a keepsake.]

Stewart K. Riddick Esq.
Stewart K. Riddick & Partners
London N12

22 July 1981

Dear Mr Riddick,

Pardon me for being alive. You must live a very desperate life, and by the sound of your letter I genuinely feel sorry for you.

What was a simple request has become almost a legal issue, and what was said in jest to your secretary has been accepted as gospel.

I already apologised to you, and apologise to her. I can't do more than that, other than send my head on a plate, will that be all right.

Sincerely,
Spike Milligan
Baffled at the human race

P. S. Being a nice person, I will still press for an award for your building next to The Limes, I am a real bastard, aren't I?

———◆———

Brian J. Holden Esq.
Chief Executive Officer
Cromwell Hospital
London SW5

2 December 1985

Dear Mr Holden,

I would like to object to the ridiculous and embarrassing inadequate garments that your hospital supplies for people having X-rays. You should supply full length dressing gowns;

otherwise these garments are a total embarrassment, and also what makes them idiotic is the fact that they fasten at the back, and this is impossible when you are alone in a cubicle. Why they are made like this is beyond my comprehension and should be beyond yours.

I don't expect you will do a bloody thing about it, but on principle, I write when I think something is wrong.

Sincerely,
Spike Milligan

Cromwell Hospital
London SW5

9 January 1986

Dear Mr Milligan,

I am very sorry that I have not been able to reply sooner to your letter of the 2nd December. Unfortunately, it arrived while I was on vacation and somehow surfaced only recently.

The comment you make is certainly justified and having been an xray patient myself recently I would agree that a light gown does leave one feeling vulnerable and exposed and we are indeed looking at alternatives to see if we can find something better.

These particular gowns are, in fact, designed to be done up at the front to avoid the problem you mentioned but the benefit of this design feature is rather lost if our staff do not take the trouble to inform the wearers of the gowns of this intention. I certainly apologize for our staffs' shortcomings and the matter has been discussed at a staff meeting of the Radiology Department to remind them.

I do appreciate you taking the time to comment on this problem as it does enable us to correct a flaw in the service we provide. I trust that should you find it necessary to use the Cromwell again we will be better prepared to provide the appropriate standard of service.

Yours sincerely,
Brian J. Holden
Chief Executive Officer

———◆———

Brian J. Holden Esq.
Chief Executive Officer
Cromwell Hospital
London SW5

15 January 1986

Dear Brian,

So, it sounds like I get the same bloody gown again.

Sincerely,
Spike Milligan

———◆———

The Editor
The Readers Digest

17 November 1975

Dear Sir,

For your College Rag page the following story might be worthy of your £50 offer for an anecdote.

An officer who I met during the war Lieutenant Reginald Davies told me of a time when he was at Jesus College. During the Christmas Vacs. he alas stayed on as he had nowhere to go. On Christmas morning he awoke in his room all alone and proceeded to carry out the following joke. He 'phoned the gatehouse of Jesus College and the old attendant answered the 'phone and said 'Jesus'. Whereupon he heard a voice sing 'Happy Birthday to you'.

Sincerely,
Spike Milligan

————◆————

Telegram to: Paul McCracken
The Manager
Gresham Hotel
Dublin

11 May 1993

I believe the suite I am to stay in is now called the Elizabeth Taylor Suite, will she be there. Would you ask her to take up a bacchanalian position in the brass bed.

I ask one significant question what has she ever done for
Ireland certainly not me.

WR
SM

[After all that, he didn't get the suite.]

———◆———

The Chairman
Harrods Ltd
London SW1

26 January 1966

Dear Sir,

I am being badgered into paying the enclosed bill. I decided to
pay this bill at the same rate at which Harrods did the job, overall
it took two years from the first phone call until the final
completion of the job during which time I spent no less
than 24 of my working hours attending workmen on the site
who had come with insufficient instructions and also left all their
paraphernalia in the front garden after the job was finished.

No I will pay this bill in the way I think fit and if you wish to
take me to court I have a complete analysis of the work and I will
be only too glad to let the press know how the work was done.

Yours faithfully,
Spike Milligan

———◆———

[Spike wasn't allowed to sign contracts. This was him in mischief mood.]

5.   I acknowledge that I am appearing on the programme
     as an independent contractor and that I will be
     responsible for the payment of all taxes contributions
     and levies applicable to the payment to be made to
     me hereunder

6.   I indemnify you, W-F Productions Inc and Group W
     Productions the sponsors and broadcasters of the
     programme and their agents and all other persons or
     entities connected with the programme against any
     liability caused by the breach of the rights of any
     person or entity arising from any statement act
     pose or routine made or performed by me during the
     programme

                                   Yours faithfully

Name .... X Spike Milligan X   Pope Pius III
                                       ....
                                          Signature
Address..... Spike Milligan Productions

        ..... 9 Orme Court ....

        ..... Bayswater W2 ...

[Typical telegram. The game: guess the date.]

[Buttons arrived in the mail to Spike without a letter.]

[Smarty pants.]

[Spike was questioned going into Spain. Passport photo had a beard. By the time he went to Spain he was clean shaven and there was a dispute about allowing him entry.]

Tony Aspler Esq.
Sunday Times Magazine

4 May 1970

Dear Mr Aspler,

I am sending two of my passports. One taken in Naples. 'See Naples and die!' they say. My photograph verifies this belief, and shows me 'Lord Byron' like on the point of death.

Passport photograph number two shows me having recovered from death in Naples, and due for an encore. Note the despair with the beard. It cost me a headache. When I presented it to the Spanish Authorities, I was clean shaven. They kept me under house arrest until the beard grew long enough to match the despair photograph, by which time my holiday was over.

Give Franco the rock! I say. Right on his bloody head!

Yours sincerely,
Spike Milligan

Brisbane

Sir,
    Metric Madness!.. W. Finlay is right!
(Aust 8 May) I used to be 5 Foot eleven
inches, now I don't know what I am!
                    Yours etc
                    Spike Milligan

P.S This means that Sir Bernard Miles
    must now be Sir Bernard Kilometers!

[Letter to a newspaper after reading a letter from W. Finlay (unknown to Spike) complaining about metres instead of feet.]

[Note at bottom of doctor's bill:

'These accounts are prepared by microcomputer and the system can only function accurately if your cheque exactly matches the total fee shown. If in doubt please contact Fiona.'!]

Dr Martin Scurr

24 February 1982

Dear Martin,

Reference the note at the bottom of your bill. Please note that this bill is paid by a computer called Spike Milligan, and unless the figures on this cheque tally with the amount, two things will happen:

  a) you have overcharged me.
  b) or he has overpaid you, either of these will do for you.

However, if option (c) occurs, that is you have undercharged me, and (d) I pay the under-charge, it's three points to me and my computer.

Sincerely,
Spike Milligan

P. S. I saw a human being today.

[Martin was Spike's doctor, and he drove him mad, they were great friends. Spike was very fond of him.]

[He sent his personal copies of the Goon Show scripts to auction. This was his note to Christie's.]

Mr. J. FLOYD   SALE of
                             Goon.

CHRISTIES.
   8 KING STREET.
        ST. JAMES'S. LONDON.
                   S.W.1.

I DONT UNDERSTAND YOUR
CATALOGING. I THOUGHT IT
SHOULD HAVE READ
15 VOLUMES OF PRINTED
LOO PAPER.

                 SPIKE MILLIGAN

[Elton John bought the scripts, and Spike was delighted. 'They've found a good home from one neurotic to another.']

2

Hobnobbing

10 Downing Street
Whitehall

26th October, 1964.

Dear Spike Milligan,

    I am writing to you because
I know where to find you. But
thank you all for your telegram
and your congratulations.

    · I hope you have no plans to
turn me into a parrot in a cage.

                    Yours sincerely,

                    Harold Wilson

Mr. Spike Milligan,

⟨ Barbra Streisand ⟩

June 22, 1966

Dear Spike,

    I loved your letter and
I think you would be a sensation
on Broadway.

    Go! Come! I look forward
to seeing you in New York.

Best,

Barbra

Mr Robert Maxwell MC, MP
Centre 42 Appeal
London W1

21 April 1965

Dear Robert Maxwell,

I write to tell you how delighted I am on your becoming
Treasurer to the Council of the Management of Centre
42 Appeal.

I, myself, had almost lost faith in the financial hierarchy, who
seldom seemed to assist real, new and exciting ideals. Normally
the financial wisemen, only concern themselves with scholastic
appeals or introducing massive finance for art galleries and other
popular prestige occasions. I am glad to welcome you down to
earth again.

Yours sincerely,
Spike Milligan

c/o Peter Rawley
24 Denmark Street,
3. 11. 66

Dear Spike Milligan.

I saw you
show last night for the second
time, and just wanted to say
that I enjoyed it even more than
on the first occasion. You are
a very funny man and you have
a marvellous imagination,

Ever,

Tom Courtenay

P.S.
The cast were
all excellent.

Tom Courtenay Esq.
c/o Peter Rawley
London WC2

7 November 1966

Dear Tom Courtenay,

Thank you for your letter; of course it comes better from
somebody of your professional standing, then one knows the
praise is given in a professional sense and, therefore, much more
valuable.

Perhaps we could meet and have lunch one day, or dinner after
the show, just to chat.

Regards as ever,
Spike Milligan

———

Peter Brook
London W8

4 April 1967

Dear Spike,

Of course it's true, of course you won't believe it.

I am going away for several months this week but hope to see
you when the right wind blows.

And I would love it to blow us into work together.

Love from Natasha,
Peter Brook

Peter Brook Esq.
London W8

5 April 1967

Dear Peter,

I can't help but laugh; did you really mean it when you said 'I am going away for several months this week', how you can get several months into one week is a phenomena, the secret of which I would like to know.

Love from Spike and Natasha

———◆———

9 Orme Court,
LONDON. W. 2.

22nd May, 1967

Peter O'Toole Esq.,
Guyon House,
98 Heath Street,
LONDON. N.W.3.

Dear Peter,

I read two things about you, one you are making a film, and two you have hurt your back; I will take the first thing first.

I think I would like to get into films but I don't seem to know how. Nobody comes near me and I am wondering if I have theatrical leprosy. I have waited for people to offer me parts and all that jazz but just nothing happens.

When I read you were making your own film I thought I would start to do a bit of personal grovelling.

Briefly, I am willing to play any part, big or small, for no money at all, just to prove I can do it, so if there are any small parts, be they straight or comic, in any of your own productions, please bear me in mind, body, legs, knees and feet.

Two, the bad back, I know a first class fellow called Dr. Kenneth Underhill who is an osteopath and his telephone number is PAD. 3124.

I'm not a bad sort of fellow really, am I?

                                Regards, as ever,

                                        Spike Milligan.

P.S.   I SAW GOD ON THE BUS

———— •■• ————

                                        Peter O'Toole
                                        London NW3

                                        1 June 1967

Most Spikey,

I will cure you of your theatrical leprosy. I will be standing
behind a camera shouting and shrieking and bullying everybody
(because I feel it's my turn) next year with a film of Brendan
Behan's only novel 'THE SCARPERER' and I shall make a
definite point of bellowing abuse at you.

My orthopaedic surgeon who deals with slipped discs tells me
that most of his clients are osteopaths.

You are a lovely sort of fellow.

Yours, in the Blood of the Lamb,
The Reverend O'Toole, S. J.

P. S. There must be two Gods because I got pissed with one the
    other night and he's never been on a bus.

———— •■• ————

Peter O'Toole Esq.
London NW3

2 August 1967

Dear Peter,

You won't forget me, will you?

Regards,
Spike Milligan

———◆———

Peter O'Toole
London NW3

11 August 1967

Dear Spike,

No.

Regards,
Peter O'Toole

———◆———

Peter O'Toole Esq.
London NW3

17 August 1967

Dear Peter,

Good.

Regards,
Spike Milligan

P. S. Like what's with this green ink man, don't tell me you are
    going mouldy.

Johnny Speight Esq.
Middlesex

18 June 1968

Eric and I have agreed we would like to do a Comedy Playhouse,
based upon him being a North Country Foreman at some kind
of works, and I a Pakistani, who works under him.

This is a love hate relationship. The Pakistani lives in the same
house and fancies Eric's daughter, and, of course, comes the
question of 'I don't want my daughter to marry a black man'.

Anyhow, we thought if you would like to write it, and needless
to say we might add one or two touches ourselves – just so you
don't get all the glory!

Regards, as ever,
Spike Milligan

HATTIE JACQUES.

20ᵗʰ Nov 1968

Darling Spike,

Just to say thank you so very much for the loan of your lovely picture, apart from being a great attraction at the exhibition it gave me enormous pleasure to gaze upon it for a few days, you are such a talented gentleman its almost sickening, and yet you are a good cook too!

We raised about £2,000 for the Leukaemia Research Fund, I'm still jumping up and down on the spot and grinning from ear to ear.

Thanks again, dear Spike for your help.

Love
Hattie

Miss Hattie Jacques
London SW5

25 November 1968

Dear Hattie,

Bad news; I am not a good cook. Thought you ought to know as early as possible before you start sending me empty plates to fill.

It was great news about the money you raised.

Regards, as ever,
Spike

16 December

Dear Spike

Thank you so very much for
sending me the Australian book which
has accompanied me to the comparatively
easy life here in Switzerland whereof I
propose to play with snowballs until the end
of Jan. So alas I have missed the
second coming of the bed sitting room &
I shall have to catch you in O'Casey.
At least that is what they tell me you
are up to next.

So have a happy new year
— assuming that you have already had
an appropriate Christmas.

All the best
James.

David Shepherd

Surrey

Nov. 4ᵗʰ.

Dear Spike —

Just off to San Francisco to auction the painting — we may even get the helicopter (26000 quid) in one evening if all the hob nobs are sufficiently drunk before the bidding begins ! — anyway — many thanks for the second book of poems. (the first is one of the most 'read' books (the four shepherdesses' possess — they <u>adore</u> it) __

best regards —— *David* .

LIONEL BART

Mr. Spike Milligan,
9 Orme Court,
LONDON W.2.

23rd December, 1969

Dear Spike,

Upon the idea that I should do some songs for your adaptation of "UBU ROI" (how about that title?) - I would like to cast my blessings - good ones.

I have only read several pages of the copy Sean K gave me, and I know I would like to play on it with you all - if that idea makes you pleased.

I haven't done anything remotely like this since "FINGS AIN'T WOT THEY USED T'BE" at Stratford East with Joan Littlewood. If the making of "UBU ROI" turns out to be as much fun as was the making of "FINGS" with Joan and her ensemble; then, I'm looking forward to us getting team-handed as soon as possible. (Come to think of it - Large Oscar Loewenstein was responsible for getting me together with Littlewood for that auspicious occasion. It's always nice to have someone big and strong to lay the responsibility on).

Meanwhile, I'm sending you a copy of a gramophone record that I wrote and made mouth-music on to, some sixteen months ago. I want to give it to you as a Christmas present. I also hope to see your face when Sean and me get back from Morocco.

Regards,

Lionel Bart

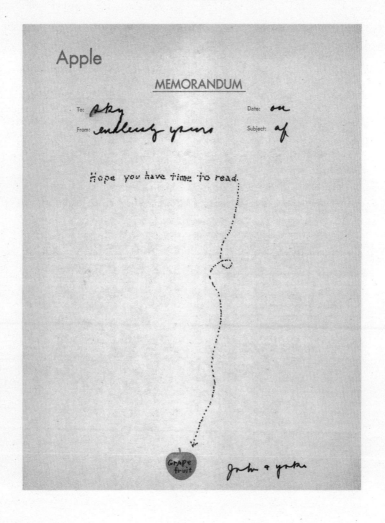

Barry Humphries Esq.
Melbourne
Australia

1 June 1970

Dear Barry,

How nice to find out that you left the country without saying Goodbye.

I presume the reason is so you can use my name and have your own series called The Spike Milligan Show in Melbourne.

Anyhow, are you coming back? If you are, let me know when because I have an idea for a series which I think could be both remunerative and funny.

Needless to say, you will get Top Billing and my name will be in small print at the bottom.

Let me know.

Love, light and peace,
Spike Milligan

———•———

LONDON N. W. 3

10th June,1970

Spike Milligan Esq.,
9, Orme Court,
London,W.2.

My dear Spike,

What a nice comforting person
you are. I am sorry you did not think
much of my predecessors but I am glad to
know that you think I was better! I did
love the Ministry of Housing and particularly
the work on historic towns and buildings.
And it was good to feel that we were able
to do one or two useful things together.
I am busy re-orientating myself at the
moment but it will be nice if we can lure
you both over one evening for dinner.

With love to you both,

Yours

Anthony Greenwood

André Previn

10 January 1972

Dear Spike,

I loved your poem a lot. Once, years ago, Ira Gershwin wrote me a verse inscription in his book of lyrics using the same flattering rhyme from my last name. At that time, he pointed out that Aneurin Bevin was the only other possible rhyme and that he had rejected it. I hope that you rejected Bernard Levin as summarily. I can't rhyme 'June' and 'moon', so the only way I can get even is to set your poem for soloists, massed chorus, the LSO and solo trumpet which you can then perform with us.

I really liked it. Thank you.

André Previn

Sir Harry Evans
Editor
Sunday Times

17 January 1973

Dear Sir Harry,

Congratulations on the Newspaper of the Year award, you deserve it. I myself have decided to give you a knighthood.

See you soon.

Love from
Spike

Dear Spike,
         I have sent a donation
today to the Wild Otter Trust — but more
important than that I would like to
say to you that you are an amazing
person, and may God bless you for all
you do in so many directions — you are
a great Soul in a world of Ass Holes!
   If you are ever in Henley — you are
always welcome for a ~~cup~~ of Tea.
              Love from
                    George
                         (Harrison).

ॐ ✝

[Written to Sir Michael Edwardes when he received the £990m grant from the Government.]

Dear Michael.

Lend us a quid. !

Regards

Spike (millyal)

Dear Smike,

Attached . One got

£990m or so — please

therefore but dream of

paying it back !

Michael .

———◆———

Bing Crosby
c/o Franklyn Konigsburg
International Famous Artists
9255 Sunset Boulevard
Los Angeles 90069
California
USA

20 February 1974

Dear Bing,

Just to tell you that I am very glad you got over your illness because if you had kicked the bucket it would have been a great chapter in my life written off.

I really started my career when I first heard you sing 'Down the Old Ox Road' (it never became a hit but you did).

I remember I had never been so excited for years as when I introduced you on the Eamonn Andrews talk show a few years ago and my God, you floored me when you remembered 'Our Big Love Scene' and for me to get excited at the age of 53 is really something.

I am sending you a book I wrote about Ireland knowing you like me are an ex patriot Irishman.

Love, light and peace,
Spike Milligan

Clive James Esq.
The Observer

3 December 1975

Dear Clive,

You've done it now – having been declared a genius by you, my wife makes me get up and make my own breakfast. She says to me 'You're the genius, you bloody well make it'.

But I am very grateful to you because the first Q5, I thought had been forgotten completely, and no attempt was made to export it overseas, but I think your write up (and BBC do take notice of write ups) might have made a little headway getting overseas.

This is not a grovelling letter, just a thank you.

Love, light and peace,
Spike Milligan
Dictated by Spike Milligan over the telephone and
signed in his absence

John Bratby. ara. arca. rba. fial. FRSA

12 May 77

Dear Sheke.

Thanks for the invite to supper. Am painting the head of the Dept of Health & Social Security this afternoon & early eve.

Yesterday Painted Mick McManus. Tomorrow Leonard Murray.

And you?

We'd love to come to supper another time

wedding day falling over wound!

blind to the ways of the world.

clear brow with no corrugation of superficial frowns & triumphs, as in unworried second childhood

20 year old spectacles.

48 year old spectacle

100 year old joke.

Special beard with open spaces

Love John

Ronnie Scott Esq.
Pete King Esq.
Ronnie Scotts Jazz Club
London W1

31 March 1981

Dear Ronnie, Dear Pete, or anybody who is listening,

What can I say about that evening at Ronnie Scotts listening to Buddy Rich? I have a theory now, that the people who were sent to extermination camps during World War II had been given a choice they would say 'Do you vant Auschwitz, or that fucking awful table that Ronnie Scott gave to Spike Milligan at the Buddy Rich concert?' Please let me know next time I have bought a ticket for Auschwitz, as the next Buddy Rich concert gets nearer and nearer, the queues for Auschwitz are getting longer and longer. In fact, I think one of the people in the queue is Buddy Rich, he can't stand it either.

Let me put it this way, if that table was a suit, I would look like a fucking cripple. Whoever invented that table invented a guide dog for the deaf.

Do you know that Ringo Starr hangs around outside John Lennon's apartment wearing a bullseye over his heart, he is determined to make it somehow.

Look Ronnie, you really could have gone the whole hog why didn't you put that table in the centre of the door, leading to the dressing rooms. Think of the funt it would have been hurgling.

I await your usual fucking silence.

How can you both become members of the Wig and Pen Club?

As ever,
Spike Milligan

Memo from Barry Humphries

Barry Humphries is a division of the Barry Humphries Group

To   Spike Milligan, Esq.
Subject   *The Art of A. H. Fullwood*

Date   *9 Nov. 1983.*
Copy   *Alan Clare*
         Bob Todd
         John Bluthall

Dear Spike,

Nearly a year ago Dame Edna Everage's security guards clashed with your own outside a Birmingham book-shop. Couldn't we meet privately soon, without an entourage of hostile heavies?

I am re-married with two young children and I would like you to kiss them, so you can one day tell your grandchildren: 'Barry Humphries asked me to kiss his kiddies'.

I am addressing this to Orme Court and I hope that Peter Rawley or Beryl Virtue will re-address it.

I think I owe you a Greek lunch.

Love
Barry Humphries

The recipient is advised to preserve this memorandum as it could well become a very extremely valuable collector's item.

Barry Humphries Esq.
London SW7

15 November 1983

Dear Mr Everage,

Your wife has somehow got my address, I have been trying to avoid her for the last 20 years. She believes actually that her security guards, and my security guards clashed in Birmingham, indeed it is possibly one of the best areas for security guards to clash, the climate is mild and the people impoverished. Actually the occasion I remember, I was trying to get you there to show you how pitiful and poverty stricken it was, and as depressed as Moonie Ponds, where she left some 20 years ago to live a life of package tours, and artificial pearls, and National Health spangled glasses. I know for a fact she has varicose veins, piles and wears an appliance, she's had several face-lifts over the last year, which has improved the plastic surgeon's income and little else. But, of course, Norman, I will be delighted to meet you, I suppose that it is her conscience that's bothering her, I mean I knew her when she was alive, and believe me but for her pacemaker, she wouldn't make it to the dunny.

These are my movements: at the moment I am in Southsea, for the week, week of 21st November, Norwich, week 29th November, Slough, week 5th December, Wimbledon, week 12th December, Brighton.

I actually think that Prince Charles is coming to have dinner with me in January or February at my home in Barnet, if you would like to be there on that occasion do let me know, and, of course, I will order up a bottle of Borossa Pearl for that occasion and some lamingtons.

Do phone Norma Farnes at my office, 727 1544, and give her a date when we can meet.

Love, light and peace,
Spike Milligan

c.c. Dame Edna Everage
Old Matron's Home
Woy Woy

———◆———

Warren Vache
New Jersey
USA

25 September 1986

Dear Warren,

Thank you for your note of sympathy in the Key of G. Alas I was suffering a slipped disc in 5 sharp, one of the world's most agonising keys; by being a natural arranger I transposed it to B flat for the piano, putting the illness in the key of C.

For a full report on the agony phone (01) 441 1522 and unless I am much mistaken, I will answer you.

Keep playing man.

Love, light and peace,
Spike

———◆———

Mr W. Vache
New Jersey
USA

5 May 1988

Dear Warren,

How very kind of you to miss my birthday by 17 days. I hope
your sight reading is better than this, another thing, why are you
persecuting me like this, with long distance phone calls from the
colony of America.

I am sorry to tell you this but your eyesight woefully needs
testing, you see I am a negro and I want you to be the first to
know. Its just that I was born a negative and when I was
developed I went white, but I think by the time I see you again I
will have had a body transplant, I am going for Sophia Loren's
then I can go to the pictures by myself.

Warm Regards,
Spike Milligan

<hr />

Paul Getty Jnr
London SW1

12 January 1988

My dear Paul,

When I 'phoned you the other day, in a joyous voice you said 'I
have been out'. My dear Paul out could be the in thing. I mean it is
ridiculous of you to tell me on the 'phone that you are in, and not
'out', one is the case of being there and the other is the case of not.

I mean out can be a losing streak, for instance a man lying prone on the canvas hears '8, 9, 10 out', it would be silly for him to hear '8, 9, 10 in'. I mean it would deceive a boxer no end if his hands raised above him he was told he was not in.

I am just warning you to be careful when you are out, for instance I knew a Count who was out for the, i.e. out for the count. I mean if you are out for the count you don't hear it. You understand.

I must finish this letter now because I am going out. I will 'phone you next time you are in.

Love,
Spike Milligan

Paul Getty Esq.
London SW1

2 March 1988

Dear Paul,

I woke up this morning and discovered it was Wednesday I thought I would pass this information on to you.

Love,
Spike Milligan

P. S. I do hope you are better.

Paul Getty Jnr
London SW1

23 March 1988

Dear Paul,

You write to me on a Monday and tell me yesterday was Sunday.
I am not interested in yesterdays, for like my first and second
wives they have gone for good.

I tell you again today is Wednesday, can't you get it through
your head.

Regards,
Spike Milligan

P. S. Please acknowledge Wednesday.

———◆———

7 July 1988

Dear Mr Gorbachov,

As somebody who has been living between the great political
competition between America and Russia since the last war, may I
say out of all of it you have become a strong beacon of hope and I
think apart from that Russia will benefit greatly from your
decisions. Already from your actions Russia is not being looked
upon with the suspicion and resentment it had been since W.W.2.

I congratulate you on your wonderful enlightened approach to
a difficult subject.

In case you wonder who I am, I am an Irish genius.

Spike Milligan

———◆———

HRH The Prince of Wales KGKT
Buckingham Palace

11 October 1988

Dear Prince Charles,

I have just received an invitation to your Birthday Ball. Of course
I will come but can I have the first waltz with you? It's 1-2-3 1-2-3.
If you do 1-2-3-4 it means you get there first.
    I will see you at the snacks counter.

Love, light and peace,
Spike Milligan

------•------

Telegram to Anna Ford at the BBC sent on
Wednesday 15 November 1989

Dear Anna,

I don't like you with your hair back
Please put it back again.

Love,
Spike

------•------

Anna Ford
BBC
London
W12

19 April 2000

Dear Anna,

Did I once take you out to dinner and try to make love to you, or did I imagine it all.

   Do put me out of my misery.

Warm regards,
Spike Milligan

———◆———

British Broadcasting Corporation Room 1640 BBC News Centre Wood Lane London W12 7RJ

BBC News

One O'Clock News

20 April 00

Dear Spike.

I'm sure I would have
remembered such a momentous
event – so I *can* put you
out of your misery.

But I do remember
having dinner with you
(many years ago) in a little
Italian restaurant in
Kensington, chaperoned by
T. Wogan Esq.

Warm regards to you
too, Dear Spike,

Anna   x.

[Spike protecting his best mate after Eric had had a row with Ray Cooney. I just love it.]

17 April 1990

Dear Eric,

Ray Cooney is a cunt – I wouldn't put myself out of work because of a cunt. I would continue as is and ignore the cunt. I wouldn't let the cunt deprive me of nearly £3000 a week. He can't do anything except insult you, he can't fire you.

So, you go on letting him be a cunt and you get paid £3000.

Your very old and wise friend,
Spike Milligan
and the Samaritans

Germaine Greer
c/o The Oldie

4 February 1993

Dear Germaine,

Regarding the Archers at Crecy here is an extract from the Art Of War In The Middle Ages 'The welsh marcher Lords were assessed at another 3350 men, half spearmen and half *archers*'. Marry me.

Love,
Spike Milligan

Germaine Greer
Cambridgeshire

29 April 1993

Dear Germaine,

I am sending you a copy of my poems Hidden Words, I mean somebody has got to read them. I have got the other one and the third is in the possession of the South African police.

Whatever are you doing these days you seem to be living in a chicken house with some goose eggs and forever planting trees in high winds.

I am sorry they were Greek archers at the battle of Crecy come to think of it I'm sorry there were English archers as well because the Welsh could have won it without them.

Why did you marry Kingsley Amis? You must never do it again, I would have been a much better choice as I have the unexpurgated version of the Karma Sutra.

Love, light and peace,
Spike Milligan

[Robert Carrier had a TV programme on cooking food in people's houses. Spike was totally bowled over by him and told him so.]

Robert Carrier Esq.
London SW7

15 November 1994

Dear Robert,

This is rather a delayed letter. I just wanted to tell you what a pleasure it was to meet you. I found you a very commanding figure and very charismatic and, of course, that dish you cooked – what can I say it should have been under a glass case in a museum.

   Anyhow very warm regards if ever you are passing by you are most welcome to stay the night.

Regards,
Spike Milligan

P. S. As for you being in the SAS in the war I have nothing but admiration for you, I will do my best to have a special medal struck for you.

Sir Harry Secombe
Surrey

20 August 1998

Dear Harry,

Thank you so much for your book – I suppose now you want me to read it.

Love, light and peace,
Spike Milligan

———•———

Mrs Kathryn Colvin
Foreign and Commonwealth Office
London SW1

4 July 2000

Dear Mrs Colvin,

Would you thank The Queen for appointing me a KBE. Can you tell me what shape it is and what it is made of – leather, cardboard or metal? Do you carry it in your pocket or wear it around your neck with a piece of string?

Anyway, I think the reason she gave it to me was that they looked in the Obituary Column and saw that I was not in it and thought it was time to give it to me.

Thank you for sending it to me, but only just in time.

Yours most sincerely,
Love, light and peace,
Spike Milligan

3

Politely Declined

Sir Harry Secombe and his centre

11 January 1983

Sorry I can't make it tonight owing to a previous commitment, I forget her name for the moment, will be forwarding it to you in good time.

Love light and peace, Spike Milligan

P. S. They are naming a new carsey after me at the Woolwich Royal Artillery Academy. It is being called Spike Milligan Shithouse. Free seats can be arranged through this office. Book now before the dysentery season.

———◆———

[William said he would lay on raw carrots at the lunch if Spike attended. Spike and his vegetarian bit.]

7 January 1971

William Davis Esq.
Punch

Dear Willy,

Sorry couldn't make the lunch, keep trying. Regarding your P. S. why lay on raw carrots, a divan is by far the more comfortable.

Love, light and peace,
Spike Milligan

METROPOLITAN POLICE—MEMO

Spike

Please get a petrol cap, it's very dangerous to have a rag poking out.

Rank .... No. .... Divn. ....
Date ....

Harrow Road Police Station

1 September 1978

Dear Lads,

The petrol cap was knocked off during the carnival. I hear some of the lads had their caps knocked off as well. Drop in any time for tea, you are always welcome. Despite the knockers you are the best.

As ever,
Spike

Metropolitan Police
Harrow Road Police Station
London W9

4 September 1978

Dear Spike,

Sorry about the petrol cap.

To help you to get over the loss I wonder if I can tempt you to our Senior Officers Luncheon Club on Monday, 2nd October, 1978 at Paddington Green Police Station.

We are hoping it will be something of a 'celebrity' gathering. I have heard the names Harry Secombe and Jack Warner being mentioned with bated breath.

If you would like to come (as the guest of the Harrow Road Police Senior officers), we would be delighted.

Can I assure you that you would not be expected to 'sing for your supper.' We usually have a few drinks beforehand and a quite informal lunch terminating about 3 p.m.

If you can accept I will confirm the details later. If you can't come then perhaps some other time?

Regards,
C. F. Dinsdale
Chief Superintendent

Chief Superintendent Colin Dinsdale
Metropolitan Police
Harrow Road Police Station
London W9

11 September 1978

Dear Chief Superintendent Dinsdale

This is the situation. I would dearly love to get a free dinner on the Senior Police Officers on 2 October, but I fear you will have to give me a very long knife and fork because I will be in Tunisia that day planting a tree in a graveyard in Monistar (please believe me, it is all true).

Anyhow, don't let this deter you from asking me in future as hunger is one of my specialities.

Love, light and peace,
Spike Milligan

P. S. Did you know policemen are numbered in case they get lost?

Martin Leigh Esq.
Education & Welfare Officer, & Festival Committee Organiser
University of Keele
Students Union

14 June 1983

Dear Friends,

I write this letter within one hour of arriving back from Australia. Owing to the sheer weight of work ahead of me, I can't accept your generous offer to open the Keele Festival Week, or attend the Summer Ball, my own personal summer balls are about to drop off.

Hope you have a great time, I will keep fighting for lost causes.

My regards to all the Students, tell them the main problem is population.

One of them,
Love, light and peace,
Spike Milligan

———— ◆ ————

Laurence Broderick Esq.
Thane Studios
Bedfordshire

5 July 1983

Dear Laurence,

Oh that I have the wit to appreciate this situation. The day on which you are exhibiting, I am having an operation on my eyes, I could attend with a white stick and bang your sculptures around the buttocks shouting 'this sounds bloody good'.

I wish you success for the occasion.

My God, isn't the world crying out for beautiful things these days. I have been looking for a beautiful thing for quite a time now, as I haven't one of my own.

Love, light and peace,
Spike Milligan

———— ◆ ————

Anne Hillyer
Time Out

29 July 1986

Dear Anne,

I won't be up there – but Daley Thompson will, you can tell the difference he is a darker shade of pale and I am no longer a British citizen and he is.

Sincerely,
Spike Milligan

[Spike still being bitter after he had been refused a British passport. Over twenty years ago.]

———•———

Billy Connolly Esq.

9 July 1982

Dear Billy,

Unable to see you after the show owing to a severe attack of haemorrhoids. I was outraged that a man like myself who has practical haemorrhoids was not cast in your role. I know for a fact, from your army records, that you have not got piles and, therefore, I would hope you would resign this role in place of a man who is perfectly suited for the part, with an electric hand Truss, knitted by Nuns from the Poor Clare Order.

I really enjoyed the evening.

Love, light and peace,
Spike Milligan

Wilfred Josephs Esq.

9 November 1982

Dear Wilfred,

Sheer pressure of work has made it difficult for me to:
a) invite you to dinner
b) come and see you
c) ask you for money.
 I am still trying.

Love, light and peace,
Spike Milligan

Christopher Kelly Esq.
The Union Society
Cambridge

3 May 1988

Dear Christopher,

Thank you for writing to me before I died, they were just
screwing the coffin lid on when your letter came through. I can't
understand this motion that there is regret about the Roman
Empire falling, there must be some mistake, only this morning
the Tenth Legion marched through Ticehurst on their way to a
museum, none of them appeared to be falling, there's something
wrong somewhere.

Sorry I can't make it, but I didn't make Sophia Loren either.

Warm regards,
Spike Milligan

———•———

Mr A. D. Stanbridge
East Sussex

11 October 1988

Dear Andrew,

Thank you for your letter of 5th October. Alas I am not living at
Ticehurst anymore and actually I am not interested in football
ever since I had my head split open by one. Since then the rain

has been coming in and I have no roof to my mouth and I have spent my time drowning.

Sorry about the disappointment.

Regards,
Spike Milligan

[An invitation to attend the local football club. Spike had been living in Ticehurst.]

———◆———

General Secretary
Variety Artists Association
Twickenham

4 November 1988

Dear Secretary,

I am sorry I cannot attend the dinner on 27th December. My teeth are away being re-ground.

Sincerely,
Spike Milligan

———◆———

Tatler Publishing Company Ltd
London W1

6 December 1988

Dear Suzanne Baker (nee Stella Artois),

My manager told me about this venture in the Tatler Magazine, alas, I have suddenly become brain damaged in the knee, I have thought about it, and she has thought about it, and would you believe we both came up with the same word, NO. Sorry to disappoint you someone has to.

Thanks for the offer.

Sincerely,
Spike Milligan

I AM SORRY I CAN'T BE WITH YOU ON YOUR 90TH BIRTHDAY AS I HAVE BEEN INVOLVED IN AN ACCIDENT WITH A STEAM ROLLER AND I AM WRITING THIS UNDER THE FRONT WHEEL AS SOON AS THEY HAVE GOT IT OFF ME I WILL BE COMING ALONG AS A BOOK MARK FOR YOUR NEW BOOK.

WARNING — DON'T EAT THE FISH

LOVE
SPIKE

[Foyle's booksellers invited Spike to the book launch of Harry Secombe's autobiography.]

Cameron Robson Esq.
President
The Union Society
Cambridge

25 January 1990

Dear Cameron,

Thank you for your letter of 10th January. I would be useless at this debate primarily because I have been dead for 24 years now. Apart from that, I hate scientists and I hate artists. In fact, I hate everybody including you, do tell them that is why I am not at the debate.

Can the whole University please stand on the hour of midnight and think of me, it might cure my haemorrhoids, you never know.

Sincerely,
Spike Milligan

———•———

John Warburton Esq.
Kellogg International
Algeria

10 May 1993

Dear John,

Of course it is quite natural for people to go to Algeria and write asking for anecdotes about their father before he dies (you don't have a date for that do you) and are Kelloggs in Algeria now making Arab and Camel Kelloggs.

The only anecdote I have about your father is that he instructed us, at a camp in Tunisia where we had attacked the Kelloggs factory, and said 'Stop, do not fire on that warehouse one day it will be my son's livelihood, they are sending him there to write an obituary about my forthcoming death'.

I'm sorry I can't help you more because I don't want to.

Sincerely,
Spike Milligan
Total failure

[One of thousands of letters Spike received, asking for an anecdote to include in a book about his father.]

PART TWO
Milligan on a Mission

4

Pulling Strings

The Beatles
c/o George Martin Esq.

20 April 1966

Dear Lads,

I did write a letter to you all via the Epstein office and I have the feeling that you have not received it, so this time I am passing the letter to you via George Martin.

What it was all about was Ian MacPhail, the Head of Save the Wildlife Fund, asked me if it was possible for me to approach you with a view to doing a cabaret at the Wildlife Ball on July 1st. If you can do it I am certainly willing to throw in myself as well and as I consider this Organisation of vital importance to mankind, I was hoping you would see your way clear to doing something. In any case I would love to meet you all for a very worthwhile charity called the Make Spike Milligan a Millionaire Charity, which I think is a splendid idea.

Anyhow could you drop me a line saying you are interested in one or the other.

Regards,
Spike Milligan

Peter Scott CBE, DSC
The Wildfowl Trust
Gloucestershire

1 May 1970

Dear Peter,

No need to reply to this letter, so stop worrying.

Briefly, I did contact Harold Wilson (Prime Minister of no particular direction), and suggested that ████████████ might be remembered in the Birthday Honours. I explained the tremendous amount of work that ████ gets through in a year, and his tremendous zeal and energy, he not only works mentally, but actually goes out on 'safaris' with young children. On top of which he edits Wildlife Youth Service, writes articles, sets ups appeals for funds, all in all does a magnificent job of work.

Harold Wilson wrote back and said he would consider him. Alas, he did not include him in the Birthday Honours, but when I saw Kenny Lynch had got the OBE, it did make me think that Harold Wilson (Prime Minister of no particular direction) had got his priorities wrong.

I know Kenny Lynch and I know ██████████████, and I know damn well which one deserved the Honour.

I wonder then Peter, if you, in your capacity as our God Head, could drop a note to Harold Wilson, suggesting it might be a good thing to consider ██████████████ in the Birthday Honours.

You might also apply to him for a Knighthood for me, and a bursary of say £30,000, with access to Princess Anne, after dark.

Love, light and peace,
Spike Milligan

HRH The Prince Philip, Duke of Edinburgh
Buckingham Palace

30 September 1970

Dear Prince Philip,

It's that old Irish roue again (don't tell me you have guessed).

I have a request to make of you (no, it is not the next dance).
During Mr Harold Wilson's period of office I approached him
regarding Birthday Honours, with a view to including ████
████████ among the Awards. Alas, before I got an answer he
suffered from a severe attack of election.

I then wrote to the incoming Prime Minister, namely Ted
'Anyone-for-Europe' Heath, making the same request. Knowing
how notoriously fey Prime Ministers are I have been getting a
round robin and collecting names. Peter Scott is sponsoring like
Ian McPhail and myself.

I am writing to you, not to include your name on the list, but if
you could bear ████████████ in mind I am sure that this
name is deserving of an Award. He puts in a twelve-hour day,
and if you were to see one of his diaries you would realise that he
is doing the work of three men.

I do hope that you might be able to help in any way that you
think possible.

Love, light and peace,
Spike

P. S. Did you know that there are no laundromats in Peru?

O BE File

BALMORAL CASTLE

14th October, 1970.

Dear Spike

    If you think ████████ should get a gong I am quite prepared to take your word for it.

    Fortunately, or unfortunately, depending how you look at these things, this is a parliamenatary democracy which means that the current incumbent at No. 10 Downing Street is Gong Distributor-in-Chief aided by a, doubtless, extremely efficient administrative string of machinery. Regrettably the incumbents of the Palace are denied both the pleasure of pulling the strings and of influencing its operation in any way.

    Happy string pulling.

Philip

HRH Prince Philip, Duke of Edinburgh
Buckingham Palace

12 July 1971

Dear Prince Philip,

During the last Birthday Honours ███████████ got a gong; I don't know, if as a result of my letter to you, you had a hand in this, if you did thank you very much.

If you didn't I shall never play the Prince and the pauper with you again.

Love, light and peace,
Spike Milligan

P. S. Interesting news about you going to Hungary, I know a beauty spot in Budapest 36" 24" 36".

———◆———

The Rt. Hon Edward Heath MBE, MA, MP
10 Downing Street
London SW1

17 July 1970

Dear Mr Heath,

Congratulations on your success. That's the softener upper.
When Mr Wilson was in office I suggested that he consider ████████████ for a Birthday Honour, something in the OBE price range.
████████████ was the founder of the Panda Club, which is the junior department of the World Wildlife Fund. He works seven days a week, 12 hours a day, and is an absolute inspiration to the young people whom he serves so completely.

When Kenny Lynch got the OBE I thought it was high time that ████████ got one as well.

I do hope you will consider this in your next Honours List,

Love, light and peace,
Spike Milligan

[Spike's persistence paid off. He got one.]

———◆———

Harold Evans Esq.
Sunday Times

13 November 1974

Dear Harold,

I have just heard, via the grapevine, that you might be suing Private Eye. I know this magazine is awfully naughty and likes nothing better than stirring up trouble, and pointing evil fingers at the innocent; but I find it difficult to really get angry enough to have to sue. They do actually find facts which are true, but when they haven't got enough copy they are inclined to fish around, and say things like 'Spike Milligan is a puff, and dined privately last night with Danny la Rue, who remained dressed as a woman'. (This was true, but I'm not a puff – and I don't fancy Danny la Rue).

The thing is they don't have the sort of money to stand up to libel, and in an age when papers are folding up, I would feel sorry if they were driven out of publishing. I always treat them like rather boozy University types, at Rag. Mag time.

So, I beg you not to sue them, it's best to forget all about it, very much like Jesus: 'Father forgive them for they know not what they do'.

Anyhow, we met once as you remember, and I am still in great admiration for you for the forthright approach your newspaper has towards problems – if nothing else you can rest on your laurels for the tremendous effort you made over the Thalidomide case, without you they would have got nothing.

Anyhow, I keep threatening to have dinner with you, and I hope I will be able to do this before Christmas.

Regards as ever,
Spike Milligan

<hr />

HRH The Prince of Wales KG, KT
Buckingham Palace

8 July 1981

Dear lad! what a predicament your invitation has placed me in! I am an ardent supporter and member of *all* anti-blood sports organisations, and their committees have written requesting that I do not attend the Wedding. You know I have written to you in the past urging you to become the first person in the Royal House to reject blood sports. Your secretary replied saying 'The Prince says this is a very controversial subject'. (100 marks to you for evasiveness).

Now, I know you are a very nice lad, and we all love you very much, and I want you to know that if I don't attend the wedding, I beg you not to cancel it – just make a formal announcement from the Main Altar, 'My Lords, Ladies, etc. etc. despite Spike Milligan not being here, I'm still going through with it'.

However, I have written to all the committees concerned and said would it not be better to remain on friendly terms than offer a rebuff. That is, if ever we meet socially I could discuss blood sports in a non-confrontation manner, and who knows with Lady Di's help, we might yet make you the first President of the Royal Anti Bloodsports Society. We live by our beliefs in what is right. My Hunt Saboteurs are beaten up, sometimes seriously,

I *can't* let them down – I pray you to understand, therefore, if I don't attend the wedding. However, as a result of my letter to them, they might come up and say 'OK go'.

Now to affairs of state. As to a Wedding Present, would you like India back? or would you take Southall or Brixton as a token, they say there are some buildings still standing there. The Governors Palace is only a temporary prefab, but the tin roof appears to be reasonably sound. The Vice Regal Throne at the moment is temporarily a Lipton's Tea Chest, with a powerful cardboard backing, with a Royal Escutcheon in Wog. You can get a fine view of the riots, and they have them every day, matinees on Wednesdays. It's a great show with a cast of thousands, some of them are very High Caste. Just to be on the safe side for ascending this throne, a complete blacking up kit is available from your ADC.

Do let me know if the present is OK for you, and I will order it from Harrods.

Apart from the frivolity, do let me know you understand my predicament.

Sincerely,
Spike Milligan

———— ◆ ————

HRH Prince of Wales KG, KT
Kensington Palace

25 October 1989

My dear valuable human being,

I was delighted to see you are to make a documentary on the environment. You know that the world as it is (it's not round it's bent) and what you will say is possibly the most important thing, on this subject, you will ever have to say, so I beg of you to include strongly in this subject the crushing threat of population which lies at the base of *all* our problems. You may or may not know that the population of this country is going up by another two million by 1999 and that is only an estimate (personally I think it is much higher, say another two million on top of that).

I have thought of this problem since I was a young boy in India and watched the poverty of the masses, at that time there were 300 million in India it is now going on for a billion and four-fifths of them are now accepting living in poverty as the norm and China, despite the one child policy, rises one million a year. *Somebody* has to say something about this in strong terms. Of course, biologically and emotionally the human race has never faced up to this problem before and they have to face up to it very very soon as we are now living in injury time.

I won't preach further but believe me I have had a prophetic view of mankind since I was a little boy and I am absolutely positive I am right in what I say – I beg you to accept that, so please remember when you speak again.

No need to answer this.

Love, light and peace,
Spike Milligan
Dictated over the telephone and signed in his absence

P. S. Please excuse typing – it's not mine.

HRH Prince of Wales KG KT
York House
St James's Palace

3 June 1993

Dear Prince Charles

Many years ago I took two years restoring the Elfin Oak tree in Kensington Gardens. It has been allowed to get into a dilapidated state and nobody in any Government departments is interested in it. It is a great pity because it was a little masterpiece.

I was wondering, through the Prince of Wales Trust, if you might gather together some students who are sculptures and painters in their last year and promote them financially to restore the tree. I do not know the sort of money that it would need but I should imagine about £10,000 to £20,000 to make a good job of it.

If you can't make up your mind there is always Beachy Head.

Warm regards,
Spike Milligan

———

HRH Prince of Wales KG KT
York House
St James's Palace

1 September 1995

Dear Precarious balanced Prince of Wales,

I thought I would report on the Elfin Oak. The English Heritage have done bugger all and I am going to try and raise the money from the National Lottery. They have had a quote from a company to restore it for £60,000, it would be very sad to see the tree disappear completely.

I really was very remiss in not having the tree listed Grade II when it was completed.

Presently the tree is surrounded by a monstrous fence some 12–14ft high and it looks as if the tree is being prevented from escaping when in fact the tree is literally entirely in my hands, no one else seems interested least of all Jocelyn Stephens who promised to get money from English Nature.

Anyhow thank you for trying and now thank me for trying.

Warm regards,
Spike Milligan

Sir Jocelyn Stevens
Chairman
English Heritage
London W1

9 July 1997

Dear Jocelyn,

As you did bugger all to save the Elfin Oak perhaps you could help by having it listed a Grade 2 monument.

Warm regards,
Spike Milligan

ENGLISH HERITAGE

From the Chairman
Sir Jocelyn Stevens CVO

Mr Spike Milligan
9 Orme Court
Bayswater
LONDON
W2 4RL

13 August 1997

Dear Spike,

Thank you very much for your letter of 9 July.

I think we did a little more on behalf of the Elfin Oak than you give us credit for. My problem is that I am told that it is not technically possible for us to recommend the Oak for listing, and without it being listed we are not able to grant-aid it. We did, however, spend a considerable amount of time and effort in 1993 in providing detailed advice on its preservation and restoration at the request of the Royal Parks Agency.

Meanwhile, I have asked for further advice and will let you know if and when we can do anything further to help.

My best wishes

and sorry for being such

a bxxxxr

Yours ev

Josh

Sir Jocelyn Stevens CVO
The Chairman
English Heritage
London W1

27 August 1997

Dear Jocelyn,

Thank you for your letter. Let me put the story like this; I first approached you with a book of photographs of the Elfin Oak, which was in a miserable state, and I asked if you could help and you took the book and you mentioned that you might be able to help through the organisation English Land 'They've got lots of money' I left it at that and nothing much seemed to be happening and I thought it would be better if I did something which I did, I got Paul Getty to contribute £15,000 and Paul McCartney to contribute £15,000 I then went to the Byam Shaw School of Art and asked if some of their students would help do the modelling and painting etc on the tree and from that someone formed the Elfin Oak Trust, it wasn't me. If you say you helped, none of the Trust ever passed that message or the information on to me so there it stands.

I note your comments about my saying 'English Heritage did bugger all'; well if you did, all very well and I am grateful for it, then why weren't you at the inauguration.

Warm regards,
Spike Milligan

P. S. I will ask you again, is it possible to get the Elfin Oak listed as Grade 2.

HM The Queen
Buckingham Palace

1 June 1995

Your Majesty,

Could you consider, when the present Master of The Queen's Musick retires, the composer Wilfred Josephs. He really is a superb composer and has been far too long not recognised in the country.

I am enclosing a programme showing his tremendous output and also his biography showing his awards.

Can you please use your office as Queen to suggest him to the committee that choose the Master of The Queen's Musick.

Spike Milligan

5

Hammering at the Door

Right Hon. Margaret Thatcher
Member of Parliament for Finchley
House of Commons
Westminster

16 December 1970

Dear Mrs Thatcher,

As my representative in Parliament I am making the following appeal to you.

I live at 127 Holden Road. The whole road is, in fact, private residences with back gardens. I received information, and the situation is that they have now pulled down nos. 113 to 125. Needless to say, I thought that the buildings replacing them would be flats running along the lines of the present buildings, but no, the development includes building blocks of flats half-way down the back gardens, plus a garage even further down. This, of course, used to be known as 'back building' which used to be frowned upon by the very council which now agrees to it. The whole character of street will be lost, and also the privacy of my garden, and even motor cars will be driven through the back gardens which used to be places of refuge. I would like you to give me your opinion as to whether this is an agreeable situation, or whether my objection is valid. I have contacted the people living in Holden and to date forty of them have replied agreeing with my objection.

I am asking you as my representative in Parliament what course I must take to get this 'back building' stopped.

I would appreciate a speedy reply.

Respectfully,
Spike Milligan

———·———

THE RT. HON. MARGARET THATCHER M.P.

HOUSE OF COMMONS
LONDON, SW1

25th January, 1971.

Dear Mr. Milligan,

I understand that you have now received a letter from the Town Clerk dated 19th January, a copy of which he has been kind enough to send to me, indicating that planning permission has not been given for the erection of flats in Holden Road.

Yours sincerely,

Margaret Thatcher

Spike Milligan, Esq.,
127 Holden Road,
N. 12.

Mrs Margaret Thatcher
The House of Commons
Westminster

1 February 1971

Dear Mrs Thatcher,

I don't think I have made it quite clear what my objections are. I am not objecting to flats being built on the sites of the houses already demolished. I am objecting to the flats being built half way down the back gardens, where there were never any buildings previously. Therefore, we have a situation whether the character of the street has been ruined as far as private gardens go.

I am objecting to them building flats in the back gardens not along the line of the original buildings (though even that, of course, will break the character of the street by its modernity).

I have objections from 50 people living in Holden Road, about building back gardens, and when the post clears I will be getting objections from other people around the back of Holden Road. If the *majority* of people in the area concerned are objecting to back garden building – surely you, as MP for Finchley, should do something to represent these people's wishes.

Sincerely,
Spike Milligan

Mrs Margaret Thatcher
The House of Commons
Westminster

9 February 1971

Dear Mrs Thatcher,

Reference your letter of 25th January, yes they have turned down the plans, but not on the basis of building flats half-way down the gardens. They are only objecting to the style of the buildings so the objections that I and 50 residents of Holden Road have lodged still remain unanswered – that is, not only building flats on the lines of the original buildings, but also building in the back gardens as well.

In the light of this, my request to you still stands. As MP for Finchley, I am asking you to present the objections of 51 people in Holden Road to the Council to the plan for building half-way down the garden.

The Council already know the residents' objections but have not answered the protest letters. The Council represents the public locally but they have decided not to deal with this problem as they have not answered the letters. We are asking you to register our protest to them as the MP for Finchley.

I hope this is clear this time.

Respectfully,
Spike Milligan

P. S. But for the GPO strike, I would have had many more objections from people living in the roads around the area of Holden Road.

spike milligan

Dictated on
the phone 24.2.71.

9 Orme Court,
LONDON. W. 2.

23rd February, 1971

Mrs. Margaret Thatcher, M.P.,
House of Commons,
Westminster,
LONDON. S.W.1.

Dear Mrs. Thatcher,

I have read the Town Clerk's letter of the 19th January
and in none of the statements do they refute the potential
possibility of building in back gardens of Holden Road.
(I myself know very well that they <u>are</u> going to).   But,
so as to get the case clear, for you, I am asking them
categorically to answer the question: "If the design and
construction all meet with the Council's approval are you
willing to allow buildings to be built in the back gardens
of what were 113-125 Holden Road".

I have told them I am awaiting their reply, because I will
commit it directly to you.   As I say, I had 50 objections
from people in Holden Road, which represents most of the
people involved in these plans, but for the postal strike
I would have got more objections from people living in
the quadrangle. that runs around the back and side of Holden Rd.

You do realise if the Council are taking no heed of these
objections, then we must have some kind of representation
and in this case it will fall into your lap, as our Member
of Parliament.

I am sorry to burden you with this, but this concerns people's
future lives.

Respectfully,

Spike Milligan.

The Crocii in Kensington Gardens are lovely!

Borough Planning Officer
London Borough of Barnet
London N3

23 February 1971

Dear Sir,

Reference your letter of the 19th January, 1971 none of the points laid out in your letter state whether or not you are allowing buildings to be built in the back gardens.

Therefore, I ask you a straightforward question: if the design and construction all meet with the Council's approval are you willing to allow buildings to be built in the back gardens of what were 113–125 Holden Road.

Respectfully,
Spike Milligan

P. S. You can telephone your reply through to my Manager between the hours of 10-00 a.m. and 5-00 p.m.

———•———

Mrs Margaret Thatcher MP
House of Commons
Westminster

5 March 1971

Dear Mrs Thatcher,

I have got the Council to answer the question 'Are you going to build in the back gardens', and as I predicted the answer is yes, they are going to build in the back gardens.

Therefore, no matter how many plans they reject, for the proposed redevelopment the final one will still include buildings in the back gardens.

As I have said, most of the people in the road objected to this, and when the postal strike is over, I am certain all the people around the back will also object, so it is no good putting our objections to the Council because they know about them and are ignoring them.

Therefore, I am asking you as my MP representing the people to place our objections to the Barnet Borough Council and ask them whether they are, in fact, ignoring our objections.

I do hope you can do this for us, as you are the only person to whom we can go.

Respectfully,
Spike Milligan

THE RT. HON. MARGARET THATCHER M.P.

HOUSE OF COMMONS
LONDON, SW1

19th March, 1971.

Dear Mr Milligan

I have put the point to the
Council on your behalf.

Yours sincerely

Margaret Thatcher

Spike Milligan, Esq.,
9 Orme Court,
LONDON, W.2.

*Can't she as my M.P. Say she agrees —
or not.*

Mrs Margaret Thatcher MP
House of Commons

                                                        30 March 1971

Dear Mrs Thatcher,

Thank you for your letter and thank you for representing my objection to the Council, but what I would like to have from you is an opinion as to the fairness of the planned buildings in my road. I think as my Member of Parliament you are allowed to express an opinion on behalf of your constituency, and I think it is within your powers to say (a) you agree with their grievance or (b) you do not agree.

As I have told you, the Council are allowing a massive development right in the middle of Holden Road. Anyone with any consideration for environment would at least consider starting the development at one end and gradually working along, but to put it right down in the middle destroys the whole environment of the road.

As I have told you, not are they doing that but they are building half way down the garden and garages right at the bottom. Now I have solicited almost 100% objections from the people living around the development: this means the *majority* of your constituents object to the plans being allowed by the Council. Therefore I am asking you, are you backing our objection or are you just passing it on and remaining neutral?

I shall be glad to hear as soon as possible as to what attitude you intend to take.

Sincerely,
Spike Milligan

THE RT. HON. MARGARET THATCHER M.P.

HOUSE OF COMMONS
LONDON, SW1

5th April, 1971.

Dear Mr Milligan,

Thank you for your further letter.   I am afraid
I cannot venture an opinion.   As you may know,
when planning permission is turned down there is
a right of appeal to a Minister which he must
exercise judicially.   Bearing in mind that I
also am a Minister, it would be quite wrong for
me to express an opinion on this case.

Yours sincerely

Margaret Thatcher

Spike Milligan, Esq.,
9 Orme Court,
W.2.

*She has never once grasped or admitted the
back building.*

Write Town Clerk. What is their decision.

Write to House of Lords.

*I'm not not asking her as a Minister I'm asking
you as an MP*

Mrs Margaret Thatcher MP
c/o House of Commons

6 *April 1971*

Dear Mrs Thatcher,

You keep avoiding the issue of whether you support my application and the residents. Quite obviously you wish to remain neutral. In this respect it's a great pity.

As to the local enquiry, might I say it's not being held to decide whether they should build in the back gardens or not: this has already been decided, so I don't see any point in coming along to that enquiry. It's a very sad day when your own MP cannot support you and the residents in a perfectly legal claim. I hope you have a conscience.

Respectfully,
Spike Milligan

———◆———

Mrs Margaret Thatcher
House of Commons

13 *April 1971*

Dear Mrs Thatcher,

Thank you for your letter of the 5th April regarding the objections of the local residents and myself, as to the buildings in the back gardens. When I wrote to you asking for your help, I did not write to you as a Minister, I was writing to you as our Member of Parliament for Finchley.

In this case, we have the residents who have a justifiable grievance in which it would appear that the Council are not interested and so far the Minister for the Environment has done nothing, and, therefore, I ask you again, not as a Minister, but as the Member of Parliament for Finchley to help us.

If we cannot get help from our own Member of Parliament, where can we go? Is this a democracy or a bureaucracy.

Surely, first you are a human being and have feelings about right and wrong, and therefore as the elected Member of Parliament, you should be concerned with things that are right and wrong in your own Borough. I am appealing to you for help in trying to get a Public Enquiry. Now, it's no good telling me they are having a Public Enquiry, this I know; but the Public Enquiry is not being held to hear the objections of the local residents about buildings in back gardens.

Therefore, I ask you again, can you help us please. I can't believe that absolutely nothing is being done to help the local residents put forward a justifiable complaint.

Sincerely,
Spike Milligan

[What an incredible woman. Why didn't she just tell him to sod off?]

The Superintendent
Police Station
Harrow Road
London W2

19 April 1972

Dear Sir,

I want to report an incident.

On Sunday 2nd April, 1972, at approximately 4.30 pm. I witnessed two women and a man with a Great Dane dog – the dog defecated on the pavement.

I followed the people who went to Queens Mews.

I wrote to the Westminster City Council and they told me I should report the incident to the Police.

As the streets of Bayswater are polluted excessively by this disgusting habit I do hope we can prosecute.

Respectfully,
Spike Milligan

———◆———

Inspector Haines
Harrow Road Police Station
London W2

16 May 1972

Dear Sir,

Milligan versus Dog Shit Case Number 2

On Sunday the 7th May at about 11.30 am. a large black dog defecated on the pavement, I called the creature and said 'Come here Darling', and saw that its label bore the address – Burnham Court, Moscow Road, and the dog's name was Liz. A fitting Royal name for a debasement of the Royal city.

Would you please prosecute?

Sincerely,
Spike Milligan

———◆———

Memorandum
Norma Farnes
Spike Milligan

31 May 1972

Inspector Haines from Harrow Road Police Station called in to see you today regarding the letter you sent him: 'Milligan versus dog shit case no. 2.'

He personally is going along to Burnham Court to see the owners of the dog Liz. And give them a warning. He said he thought it best to go and give them a warning without prosecuting first. Because you would have to go to court and give evidence, and he thought it best to give them a warning. However, if you want to prosecute will you contact him.

(n) No don't prosecute – but do warn.
What about Dog Shit No.1? (S)

———◆———

Memorandum
Norma
Spike

23 June 1972

Inspector Haines from Harrow Road telephoned regarding Dog Shit No. 1 and Dog Shit No. 2.

He has been and warned both of these people.

He said what about Dog Shit No. 3 !!

———◆———

The Rt. Hon. Michael Foot MP
London NW3

2 August 1983

Dear Michael,

I write to you on the occasion of you relinquishing your position as Leader of the Opposition. Needless to say, I was sad that the Party never made it through the Election.

Even though by nature I am labelled as a clown, I now know at the age of 66, I have been gifted with perspicacity, to read pretty clearly the emotional state of the people of this Island; on the strength of it I know we can gain a victory.

It would be madness to go to the next Election with an identical Manifesto, what I must say, and I beg you to think of this deeply, this is no longer a purely political fight.

Growing up all around us has been a colossal environmental change, and a complete shift in the emphasis of the thinking of the working class. Briefly they now should be called the Consumer Society, they are completely dissatisfied. They see all the perquisites being hurled at them by the capitalistic world – in other words they want to be mini capitalists.

While the world of politics from 1900 has gone on its quasi Victorian way, a new and colossal problem has loomed up which has put unbearable pressure on the world of services, i.e.

Question: Why does a man with a rupture have to wait two years before he gets into hospital. The accepted political answer for that is 'We do not have enough hospitals'. Wrong. The answer should be we have too many patients/people.

Likewise, crowded trains, crowded tubes, traffic jams, even nowadays the motorways, and always the antique political answer – build more and bigger. In other words the political answer we are looking up our own arse for the answer.

I notice that hospital doctors are working 18 and 19 hours a day, sometimes going three days and nights without sleep (from my own experience), hence the level of medical efficiency has dropped in humanitarian terms. This is evident by the increased number of patients suing doctors and hospitals.

We definitely do need a stabilised population. This would not entail anything morally wrong, it could be carried out in a highly intelligent way, as Mr Lee Kuan Yew of Singapore is doing.

At the moment all politicians are bursting a gut, pointing in all directions as to what the problem is; but never pointing it towards the nigger in the woodpile, and that is population.

I realise this is an entirely new phenomenon, which politicians have never dreamed of, or prophesied, and are therefore intelligently and emotionally disinterested in it.

If this was pointed out to the working class as a whole, that their lifestyle would benefit more by restricting families to two (again as Lee Kuan Yew has pointed out) they are not stupid enough to revile this.

It will show a deep desire by the Socialists, at the fountain head, to show concern about the welfare of children even before they are born, and showing your concern for the future of families that might outgrow their own financial situation.

The small sum of this is my complaint about the traffic jams, when I realised I was never enlightened on this problem and, therefore, had four children. I now know I could have given two a better life, than I could have given four; and regarding traffic jams, they all have a car, which means I have put four cars on the road in front of me. I am saying I have made my own traffic jam. So, we make our own traffic jams, hospital jams, crowded beaches jams, crowded airport jams, and as a result of all this, people are becoming de-sensitised, they don't know what tranquility and quietude is anymore.

I can add to this an endless list, but do believe me there should be a place in the Manifesto for what I have said. If we don't do it, one day, one party will, by sheer force of numbers.

Going along with all this is the horrendous cruelty to the world of animals, battery farms – was there ever a greater obscenity.

Reduce numbers and we reduce the pressure on all of us, it's common sense, except it has never been put in a political manifesto, and it's time we did.

There's a tremendous environmental lobby growing in this country, it could be to our advantage.

I could give you lots of statistics and figures, but just believe me Michael.

Part two of the Gospel according to Milligan.

Mixing with people on a large ratio as I go around the world, I always talk to people about problems, and I notice one that was lurking among the labour voters; the right to choose if they wanted private medicine or education, and I must point out to you that on a television programme, some 18 months ago, you were consulted by a working class lady, who asked for the right to send her kids to a Private School, when she and her husband had saved the money, and you must have lost a couple of million votes, because you did waffle about the level of state school education getting better all the time, and she went away, as I did, not entirely convinced. This on a democratic basis should be allowed to the labour supporters; I am certain this lost us a lot of votes, it nearly lost mine, it was only because I am faithful to Socialism that I didn't, but then my children have already grown up, and been to Private Schools. There's millions of young Socialist couples who are going to have children, who might desire private education for their children – who are they going to vote for Michael?

Anyhow, I end this, do think about this, I know that the Socialist Party is a good idea and has good ideas, but as Hamlet said 'a good idea must give way to a better one'.

The ultimate meaning of life is that we live on a finite planet, the present political course is infinity, this is very unfair on future generations.

I hope you continue in the firebrand capacity from the back benches, as you did when Wilson was in power, which was so effective he was forced to pull you in to Government.

Love, light and peace,
Spike Milligan

———•———

The President of the United States of America
The White House
Washington DC

17 December 1998

Dear Mr President,

You can't do it! You can't torture the Iraqis with sanctions and then on top of that bomb them. Whoever is advising you is an idiot.

Yours sincerely,
Spike Milligan

6

Letters to the Editor

16 January 1964

Sir,

To date no one has explained to me the Christian value of why the College of Cardinals censured Pope John for daring to have lunch with his gardener. To my dull mind this is religious snobbery or just plain stupidity. Can anybody enlighten me?

Recently a Priest refused the Blessed Sacrament to a lady doctor (a mother of seven) for opening a birth control clinic. My brother has a photograph of Roman Catholic Priests giving the Blessed Sacrament to Italian pilots who half an hour later were bombing helpless and defenceless Ethiopian women and children. I would have thought that killing a woman would come under the heading of a form of birth control. Yet one can get the Blessed Sacrament prior to a legalised murder and yet if one dare issue a contraceptive to a poor family woe be tide us.

Can I please have an *intelligent* answer, not one from the book of rules please because that is what we are suffering from at the moment.

Yours faithfully,
Spike Milligan

The Editor
The Times

8 February 1968

Sir,

One of the last old world joys left in London was driving down
one of the last gas lit streets, Constitution Hill.

To my horror I discovered that those faceless monsters who
are gradually destroying the city, are now erecting electric lights
along Constitution Hill.

I look forward now to when they plant plastic daffodils to
match the latest vandalism.

Respectfully,
Spike Milligan

*[Spike started a campaign to save the lights in Constitution Hill. He got Prince
Philip on board and although the 'iron fingers' were being erected, he won
the battle and lampposts were reinstated. One down, a thousand to go.]*

———•———

The Editor
The Irish Times

4 March 1964

Dear Sir,

Are any efforts or any organisations in existence which are going
to preserve at least one of the buildings in which Sean O'Casey
lived during his early days in Dublin?

I am sure that future generations of Irishmen would revere
being able to see an actual building in which was once cradled

Now I know how we won the war. The formidable Milligan family: Spike's father, mother and brother Desmond.

'The Love of My Life' – Spike with Toni Pontani (she's on the far right).

Leo Milligan (father) –
like father, like son!!!

> (2) Woy Woy, 1965
>
> Place the Musket Ball in palm
> of hand & cover it with
> Powder —
>
> Frontiersman's method of measuring
> the amount of Black Powder

Leo and Florence
Milligan enjoying
the high life.

Leo and Florence aboard the
Himalaya. 'Going home.'

Met, Edgware Road, *Three Charlies*. Spike, Max Geldray and Peter.

1958. Cambridge Union tiddlywinks competition. I wonder if they won?

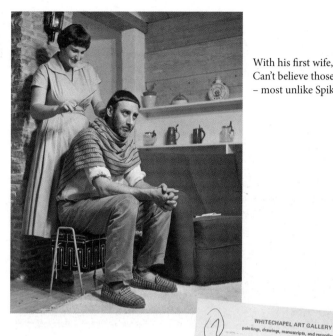

With his first wife, June.
Can't believe those slippers
– most unlike Spike.

Well, well – still in
love with the slippers
twenty years later!

WHITECHAPEL ART GALLERY
paintings, drawings, manuscripts, and recordings by

SPIKE MILLIGAN

An old man in a chair dreaming about
Bovril Sandwiches he had for tea.

S Milligan

WELL WELL STILL IN LOVE
WITH THE SLIPPERS 20 YEARS LATER!

Eric making sure Spike and Harry get it right.

Practising his Minnie Bannister voice.

Australian model, 1959. He always had an eye for the girls.

Harry's *This Is Your Life*, with Pete and Spike, turned into chaos.

Spike and Pete Sprawnsey in St Moritz. Spike still dressed from Oxfam.

The London to Brighton Car Rally, 1970. Can you imagine the language?

This photograph
haunts me because
they really were two
unhappy souls.

Was the medal from the
prop department?

Cheeky Monkey.
Son of Oblomov.

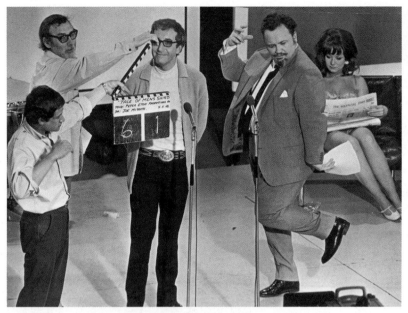

In case *The Goon Show* wasn't a success – Harry rehearsing for *Strictly Come Dancing*. Recording *Tales of Men's Shirts*, 1968.

As E. W. Mackney at Wilton's Music Hall in 1970. He loved this role.

the pen of Irish genius. All too soon these days, places which are sacred to nations are indifferently pulled down by money mad building organisations, erasing forever the sacred spot that once destroyed can never be rebuilt.

Even though Moore, Joyce and O'Casey left Dublin there is no need for the buildings they lived in to do likewise.

Respectfully,
Spike Milligan

————◆————

The Editor
Daily Telegraph

14 September 1967

Sir,

Reference your photograph and article on Highgate Cemetery, the view for it sounds ominous. I predict within five years blocks of flats will appear on it, or 'luxury type modern maisonettes'. It seems as though money has taken precedence over morality when it comes to land and houses in London and I don't seem to find anybody free from the taint.

Respectfully,
Spike Milligan

P. S. I see that a Councillor Charles Ratchford considers the cemetery an eyesore. The councils of London have been putting up eyesores in London for the past five years – I don't know what authority he has to be able to speak on the subject.

————◆————

The Editor
Sun

5 June 1968

Sir,

This attempted assassination is made even more evil, when one considers that Senator Robert Kennedy was attempting to send a bill to the American House of Representatives to stop the sale of fire-arms to civilians.

This attempted assassination seems almost like a cruel joke; I only pray that by the time this letter reaches you, Senator Kennedy will be off the critical list.

If not . . .

Sincerely,
Spike Milligan

———•———

The Editor
Daily Telegraph

12 July 1968

Sir,

The man who beats his seven year old son to death for coming home late from school (Daily Telegraph 11/7/68). He gets sentenced to 30 months imprisonment; the Great Train Robbers get life sentences, obviously loss of money is much more important than loss of life.

For God's sake, when are we going to get an equilibrate legal system.

Yours,
Spike Milligan

———◆———

[In response to one of Spike's many complaints, Davison asked Spike to be more specific about certain landmarks he would like to see protected.]

Michael Davison Esq.
Weekend Telegraph

12 July 1968

Dear Michael Davison,

OK I would like a permanent preservation order on Hammersmith Bridge, Wilton's Music Hall, the Elfin Oak Tree, No. 3/5 Porchester Terrace (this was the home of John Loudon).

Grave stone of Mrs Alice Hargreaves, who was the original Alice Pleasance Liddell, who was the little girl responsible for making Lewis Carroll put down the story he told her.

As for pulling down, literally everything built after 1929 comes in this category, with the exception, of course, of places like, Coventry Cathedral, and Liverpool, Roman Catholic Cathedral, which, at least, are positive styles, as against the faceless things that most people live and work in.

Regards,
Spike Milligan

———◆———

ose
ven in
advanced
know how

Feet in early Otello

Jan. 13.69   Times

THE ANNOUNCEMENT of the era of the odour-absorbent, disposable shoe lining has been greeted with no little relief. But before it is upon us (hopefully this summer) my remark about the yearning to shed workday shoes in mid-Verdi at Covent Garden has prompted one reader to write what might prove a useful letter for neighbours of those who succumb.

Mrs. Shirley Komrower and her husband were waiting eagerly in the front stalls for a performance of Otello in Manchester. Next to them sat a young man and older woman. "The overture had hardly started when my husband leaned right over with his handkerchief over his face and gasped 'feet'", she writes.

Moments later, she too was assailed. But Mrs. Komrower was quite up to the moment. She dashed from the theatre to an all-night chemists, bought a bottle of Airwick, and returned for her husband to place it on the floor with the wick fully extended. Soon the Airwick asserted itself, and they were able to settle down to Verdi.

PHS

The Editor
The Times

14 January 1969

Sir,

Reference 'Feet in Early Othello' (Jan 13, PHS). Indeed there is a far better invention than Airwick for stifling foot odours in the stalls during Grand Opera.

It's my own personal invention, the artificial plastic polecat. This creature is kept in an air tight zip bag, which, when opened, gives out 100% concentrated polecat fumes, guaranteed to eclipse even the worst case of foot rot.

There is a problem, of course, of offending the polecat owner, this too I have considered, by using the portable eau de cologne nosebag. These bags are secured over the nose with elastic. A small tube runs into the bag from a little round bulb carried in the trouser pocket, or ladies handbag; the slightest pressure on the bulb releases the full bouquet of eau de cologne so that the owner can watch and listen blissfully to the Opera while the patron with the foot odour is thrown anything up to 100 yards by the impact of the artificial plastic polecat.

Yours respectfully,
Spike Milligan

The Editor
Evening Standard

17 March 1971

Sir,

I couldn't agree more with Dr C. M. Fletcher on his reaction to the Government's measure of printing the words 'Smoking can damage your health'.

I can't believe that men at the top really believe that this warning is going to have any effect at all on smokers.

Nicotine is a drug far worse than pot; nicotine kills. Nicotine is the strongest common addictive in the world like gas it has crept up on us.

I have known men who had cancer of the lungs diagnosed and still could not give up smoking.

Please God send us some leaders who are not paper tigers.

Respectfully,
Spike Milligan
Dictated by Spike Milligan and
signed in his absence

Editor
Sunday Times

17 January 1972

Sir,

Atticus quotes Britain's Jingle Queen, Annie Farrow, as having thought up the catch phrase for Brooks' Surgical Supports. 'Thank you for your support I will always wear it'. I hate to break this trendy's heart, but Henry Crun first said that in a Goon Show in 1957. Later taken up by many comics, including the late David Frost.

There is to be a Cenotaph Memorial for the penultimate burial of this joke at Highgate Cemetery by my own hand. I can't leave it above ground any longer; the cannibals are too frequent.

Sincerely, etc.
Spike Milligan

The Editor
The Sunday Times

22 May 1972

Dear Sir,

> 'I can't quite take Spike Milligan
> seriously as an environment wallah
> (neither, to be fair, can he).'

> The words of your Television
> Correspondent Bevis Hillier.

By all means let him think I am not serious but please do not do my thinking for me because I am deadly serious about the subject of conservation.

Because I don't pull a long face or sound Donnish should not be taken as a portent of frivolity, because while I am working on conservation it is also for the benefit of Mr Bevis Hillier and his descendants.

Respectfully,
Spike Milligan

———— • ————

The Editor
Newsweek Incorporated

27 June 1972

Dear Sir,

'We are going to keep marching until millions of people, are brought into the Kingdom of God', (Billy Graham Newsweek June 26th).

The archaic fervour of the Missionary who campaigns more for numbers than quality, has resulted in a world groaning with Christian sects, alas, within these Societies there is no true happiness, and materialism is rampant.

Can't the well intentioned but dim Billy Grahams realise there is no shortage of Christians, just Christianity.

Respectfully,
Spike Milligan

The Editor
Guardian

14 October 1974

Sir,

Enoch Powell points out the ultimate evil of a non indigenous people (Pakistanis, West Indians etc) infiltrating, reproducing at a high rate, eventually becoming the racial majority against the natives, yet in Northern Ireland, the very people (Scots Protestants) who during the plantation *were* a minority, but proceeded by emigration and reproduction to out number the natives (Irish Catholics), are the very people he now wishes to represent.

Anybody for Volte Face.

Spike Milligan

The Editor
Catholic Herald

10 March 1975

Sir,

I was interested to read in an old Hymnal by Charles Wesley, which prefixes the books, with the words:

> 'May every Hymn in this book be sung
> always and only to the glory of God.'

Reading further in the preface we come to the line

> 'None of these valuable Hymns must be sung
> without payment of copyright fees to the owners.'

Hallelujah.

Respectfully,
Spike Milligan

———◆———

The Editor
The Times

22 May 1975

Sir,

The tragedy of the coming referendum of 'yes or no' for Europe is that people like myself who really want to note 'no', so as to retain a national identity, cannot vote 'no' because, in fact, there is no choice.

We have to say 'yes', and it is this that makes me feel we have already lost our freedom to vote 'yes or no'. We have to vote 'yes' to survive, and it is this lack of choice which I find ominous.

Respectfully,
Spike Milligan
Dictated by Spike Milligan over the telephone and signed in his absence

[34 years down the line and . . .]

The Editor
The Times

17 December 1975

Dear Sir,

One reads with alarm that the BBC are to accept sponsors for artistic events.

Among the sponsors I see who will be involved will be Imperial Tobacco – therefore, this negates the official banning of cigarette advertising on television as from the 1st August, 1965.

The Cigarette moguls must be well pleased as they can now continue on their cancerous way.

Yours etc.
Spike Milligan

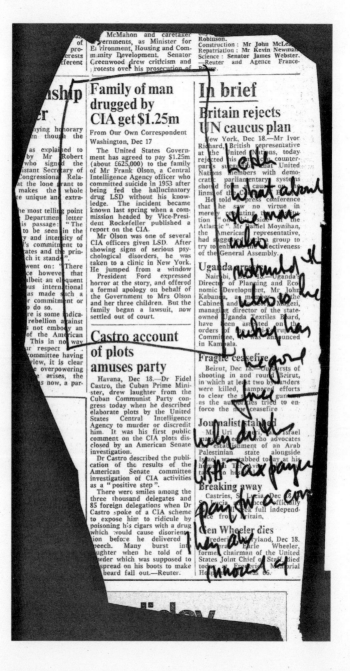

The Editor
The Times

8 January 1976

Dear Sir,

We seem to have reached an age when Christian morality is now completely superseded by a bureaucratic morality – the latter seems an ideal one for masking criminals. I refer to Frank Olson, the CIA Agent who was secretly given LSD as a result of which he committed suicide. The wonderful white-wash follow up is that the US Government agreed to pay the widow, 1.25m.

This is delightful, when the man who gave the go ahead to administer the drug, gets off scot free, the innocent American tax-payer forks out.

Yours faithfully etc.
Spike Milligan

———•———

The Editor
The Jewish Chronicle

11 September 1980

Dear Sir,

One thing has been missing in the Ceremonies concerned with Peter Sellers death, and it is one, I think, somebody should make comment about, and that is at no stage was there any attempt to introduce any connection with the Jewish side of his family. As his Mother was Jewish, most certainly then he was Jewish, whereas he did choose to be a Christian (though sometimes he

fancied various other religions), his whole attitude and
personality seemed to be that of a Jew.

Because of this I wish some small representation by the Jewish
Synagogue could have been reported or mentioned during these
Ceremonies.

There I feel better now.

Sincerely,
Spike Milligan

[Still looking after his mate.]

My Dear Mr Milligan,

I read your letter in the "Jewish Chronicle". I do not understand what you mean by "at no stage was there any attempt to introduce any connection with the Jewish side of his family" — I too, have wondered about this — after all a Jew does not usually have a funeral service in the Anglican church — you say that "he chose to be a Christian" — I had, read some time ago that his mother — of whom he was particularly attached to was a Jewess — this makes him a Jew — few people knew of his religion and obviously he did not find any pride in it — what a loss — — — his wife obviously did not think it mattered to him or else she would have spoken to a rabbi or even the Canon would have advised

2.

her properly — We jews get so much criticism that if our own — and such a talented man — prefers not to recognise his people then what can be done?

You say "there I feel better now" — well I don't know if I feel better but I hope you do —

Very Sincerely

Esther Wilson

P.S. I am just watching clips of Peter Sellers films on television — what talent ———

Mrs Esther Niren

26 September 1980

Dear Mrs Niren,

How nice of you to take the trouble to write. I am sorry you don't feel better about my letter, I think you should, as it is written by a Roman Catholic, which shows that he is concerned with the Jewish people, their tradition and their religion, which I think are among the most splendid in the world.

So, do not lose sight of the fact that at least Spike Milligan thinks the Jewish people are very very important.

It's a strange thing that in the Goon Show personnel the Goon Shows consisted of – two Jews, Peter Sellers, and Geldray, one Welshman, Harry Secombe, one Irishman, myself, a Roman Catholic, but no English. What would they do without us?

Love, light and peace,
Spike Milligan

The Editor
New Scientist

15 July 1983

Sir,

Your little snippet on the new 'Music on hold' during telephone calls; it is a continued extension, of course, of this appalling musical dysentery called Muzak. If ever there was a harbinger of George Orwell's Big Brother in 1984, this is it and chronologically he is not far out.

I have managed to equate the situation. In phoning Qantas I was put on to 'hold music' when I finally got through to the man, I said: 'Just a minute', I then sang him a whole chorus of Hey Jude, which seemed to baffle him entirely.

I tried to rationalise by explaining his Company had been kind enough to play me two choruses of some crappy music, and I was returning the compliment. If we all did this I think we might close down this pointless waste of energy.

Of course, the most meritorious level this new sound has, is the Super Loo. Without being crude, musicians' music being played in a shit-house. God what a proud day. I had heard of chamber music, but this is ridiculous.

Yours, wearing ear muffs, and a switched off brain,
Spike Milligan

Daily Mail
(Letters Page)

27 October 1988

Dear Sir,

I see that pain in the arse Kingsley Amis still continues to consider me a 'horrible Person', (Daily Mail October 27th). Well so be it. The worst thing that could happen would be for him to *like* me, that would be unbearable.

I am sending him Beachy Head for Christmas.

Sincerely,
Spike Milligan

1 November 1988
Gulag Archipelago
Siberia

Yorkshire Post

Sir,

Reference Bernard Dineen's letter about sending me to Russia.

Sincerely,
Spike Milligan
6394108

P. S. Please see the address above.

———◆———

The Independent Newspaper
The Editor

26 April 1993

Dear Sir,

With due respect to the death of Sir Ian Jacob I must make comment on your obituary. It was the occasion of when the BBC thought it very funny to get Richard Dimbleby to comment on spaghetti growing in trees a joke that only an idiot would believe and yet Ian Jacob believed it to the extent he had to look up three books before he knew it was a joke. So much for the intellect of a BBC Director General.

Spike Milligan

———◆———

The Editor
Daily Mail

15 December 1998

Dear Sir,

I read your description of the end of Barry Horne's fast and it was outrageous! This man took no nourishment for 67 days, that in itself is an epic.

The fact that he sipped orange juice – well, so did Gandhi during his fast. Is he to be condemned also? Outrageous!

Yours sincerely,
Spike Milligan

———◆———

The Editor
The Times

15 January 1999

Sir,

The Pope says God has no beard, if he knows that would he tell us what the rest of him looks like.

Spike Milligan

———◆———

7

In Defence of Animals

Miss Nora Blackborow
The Secretary
The Totteridge Manor Association
London N20

27 April 1964

Dear Madam,

I noticed this year that one of the swans on the little pond at Totteridge is without its mate. I know not whether it be the male or female who is missing. I was wondering if you would be interested in a replacement for the missing swan. I am a personal friend of Peter Scott and I am sure could arrange for a replacement, for the rather lonely looking creature that now inhabits the pond.

Yours respectfully,
Spike Milligan

Totteridge Manor Association
London N20

11 February 1965

Dear Mr Milligan,

In reply to your letter of 1st January, I am glad to tell you that the two swans are now occupying one of the Long Ponds, and we have been assured on good authority that one is a cob and the other a pen.

Yours very truly,
Hon. Secretary

———•———

The Editor
The Daily Telegraph

4 February 1965

Sir,

If your reporting is true then the case of the company director who killed a dog with a shotgun is an absolute travesty of justice. How can a man who is a company director, which takes, I presume, a degree of intelligence, pick up a gun, point it at a dog at close range and fire it and consequently killing it and then come out with such a thin argument as 'I only tried to frighten it away'. Anybody knows that pointing a gun at close range and pulling the trigger is the way to kill. How can this man get away with a £10 fine which for a man of his financial position is nothing, and on top of that to come out exonerated as a dog lover. I find the whole thing just too evident of the massive decadence in moral standards and intelligence which this Country is undergoing. Apart from everything else this man's use of the gun proves him totally unworthy of having a licence. It is tantamount to letting somebody fire a cannon at a cat to frighten it away.

Yours faithfully,
Animal Lover
Spike Milligan

━━━◆━━━

Mrs M. Thatcher
Conservative Hall

18 March 1968

Dear Mrs Thatcher,

I am writing to you asking can something be done about the unbalance between male and female Mallards in London parks.

The situation is, the males outnumber the females 10 to 1, the terrible conditions for the females during the mating season often ends up in death, mutilation, and permanent injury.

It really is the job of the Ministry of Public Buildings and Works who, and you must believe me when I say this, are incapable of any effort at all, and having formed a Committee to discuss this problem, needless to say have come out without an answer.

The answer is very simple, that is why they find it difficult to find.

We need some wildfowlers to thin down the males to a reasonable proportion. This means a little bit of office work, like writing letters to the Wildfowl Committee or Society, and asking them to come down one morning before the parks open and try and readjust the balance of nature.

The Mallards shot, need not be wasted, they can be given to the Chelsea Pensioners who, I am sure, would love them as a treat.

Please try and do something, let us see some drive in this old country which is not just made up of drains, atomic submarines, riots, retreating from outposts of the Empire. Let us try and sort some of the simple problems out as well.

Sincerely,
Spike Milligan

———•———

R. S. Teager Esq.
RSPCA

18 March 1968

Dear Mr Teager,

I am asking you for your help. The situation is, the condition during the mating season of Mallards in London Parks.

The females are taking a terrifying thrashing to the point of death, which I have seen myself. Having made a quick tour of the Parks on Sunday the females are outnumbered 10–1, 5–1, and 3–1. Something has to be done.

The solution is very simple, the males have got to be thinned out by shooting, or secondly, which would be much more difficult, trapping them at night by hand, and taking them into distant parts of the country and releasing them, which, of course, is out of the question.

The Ministry of Public Buildings and Works who should really be solving the problem are doing nothing.

I am writing around to the RSPB Peter Scott my local MP etc. We need some Wildfowlers to thin down the males to a reasonable proportion, they could go into the parks in the early morning before they were opened to the public.

Please try and help.

Sincerely,
Spike Milligan

———◆———

Peter Conder Esq.
Royal Society for the Protection of Birds
Bedfordshire

18 March 1968

Dear Peter Conder,

In the last few years, in the mating season, many Mallards in London Parks have been murdered in that the males outnumber the females 10 to 1. The result for the females is mutilation, often death, in any case very savage.

Nothing is being done at the moment. The Ministry of Public Buildings and Works, in whose lap the problem really lies, apparently are acting as if they had no lap.

The best and simplest way is getting a brace of guns, preferably Wildfowlers, who would then thin out the males in the parks, early in the morning before the public come in, and the males need not die in vain, they could find a good home on the table of the Chelsea Pensioners, any Sunday.

Do you have the necessary machinery to do this.

I am writing to various people seeking their help, Peter Scott RSPCA etc.

Please try and help.

Respectfully, earthbound,
Spike Milligan

———◆———

The Royal Society for the Protection of Birds
Bedfordshire

21 March 1968

Dear Mr Milligan

Thank you for your letter of 18th March.

I am passing your letter on to Lord Hurcomb, a Vice-President of the RSPB who can make things move. He happens to be Chairman of the Committee which advises the Ministry of Public Works on the birds in the London Parks. I will also mention this to Stanley Cramp, who is Chairman of the RSPB and also a member of the same Committee, and again who is pretty good at attempting to bully the Ministry. They both know London Parks very well.

Yours sincerely,
Peter Conder
Director

———•———

Rear-Admiral Christopher Bonham-Carter CB, CVO
Buckingham Palace

25 March 1968

Dear Rear-Admiral Bonham-Carter,

Thank you for your signal of the 20th March. I am a bit amazed, a Navy man sending signals from a typewriter, when they have a perfectly good pigeon post and heliograph atop Admiralty Arch.

The problem of the Mallard on the Round Pound is very simple.

We de-cocoon HMS Boxer, now lying at Bucklers Hard, she is dissembled, mounted on pack horses and re-floated in the Round Pound.

Using pompons, I think we can deplete the male population and send them to a watery grave (blasted foreigners).

According to the laws of Her Majesty's Parks, whereas Wildfowlers, or for that matter Unwildfowlers, are not allowed to fire guns, it is a point of Maritime Law that all watery surfaces inside 20 miles of our coast is considered fit highway for any of Her Majesty's ships.

I trust now that you will send the requisite signal to set all guns blazing on the Round Pound at dawn.

Regards,
Spike Milligan (Gunner)

P. S. You weren't ever in charge of a ship called Collingwood, were you? If so, I have got bad news for you.

———•———

House of Commons
Westminster

27 March 1968

Dear Mr Milligan,

Thank you for your letter. I knew there was this unbalance, but had no idea the difference was so great. I am sending your letter to the Ministry concerned, and will write to you again when I receive their reply. I hope in the meantime they will do something.

Yours sincerely,
Margaret Thatcher

———•———

Mr James Callaghan
Home Secretary

16 April 1969

Dear Mr Callaghan,

Just to add to your already hectic life, here's some more. I just want to register a protest regarding the Cambridge University Department of Zoology. Getting a bird and making it deaf no matter what benefit it gives mankind is just bloody barbaric. You will just have to believe me chum. If you don't know, then you shouldn't be Home Secretary.

Spike Milligan

P. S. I shall still go on supporting the Labour Party.

P. P. S. I've been in contact with Prof. W. H. Thorne, who is a nice enough chap, but bloody barbaric as I said before.

———•———

The Rt. Hon. Pierre Trudeau
Office of the Prime Minister
Ottawa
Canada

14 October 1969

My Dear Prime Minister,

I am writing to you to speak for voiceless animals, in this case, the seals, which are ruthlessly hunted for personal adornment.

I am not asking you to restrict all seal hunting, but would you like to consider making the Gulf of St Lawrence, a seal sanctuary, where they can live out their lives in security, and also add a natural attraction for parents and their children who visit that area.

Respectfully,
Spike Milligan

P. S. I am a member of the advisory committee of the World Wild Life Fund.

———◆———

The Rt. Hon. L. J. Callaghan MP
Houses of Parliament
Westminster

15 October 1969

Dear Mr Callaghan,

In the light of recent figures revealed regarding vivisection, I cannot help but as a public spirited citizen, register the degree of horror on the ever increasing number of experiments.

You really must put a break on it because, man by nature of his instinct will always ignore suffering for the sake of an experiment.

I am not anti vivisection in principle, it is rather the over increasing number of experiments which appal me.

As one of the ministers elected on behalf of the public, I, as one of them, must say I must consider this question when next casting my vote.

It would appear, neither conservative nor socialist would have any voice of opinion on this matter, which bears out my argument, that in main, man is pretty indifferent to suffering, provided it has the label Science attached to it.

I know for a fact that there are operations carried out that have very little bearing on medicine, and are done purely out of curiosity.

The recent deafening of birds at Cambridge was a point in question.

I ask you again to have re-enlightened thinking as a feeling human being and a Christian. A political answer will not suffice.

Yours sincerely,
Spike Milligan

P. S. I enclose a pamphlet which you may not yet have been besieged with. Observe it dispassionately, and you should still find it horrific.

President Richard M. Nixon
White House Office
Washington DC
USA

17 September 1969

Dear Mr President,

This is an appeal from across the Atlantic regarding the Wildlife in the Florida Swamps.

At the moment there is a threat, that the water, on which the wildlife lives and survives is being dissipated by various irrigation schemes and dredging. Of course, the wildlife is voiceless and can make no appeal, except to men with consciences and a feeling of respect for the creatures on this planet.

When man set foot on the moon it was dead, let that not happen in any measure on this planet.

I am a member of the Advisory Committee of the World Wildlife Fund and, therefore, I speak with a certain degree of knowledge on the subject.

I wish you well in your mammoth task as a new President, and hope you will bear in mind some of the small things, one of which I have brought to your attention.

Respectfully,
Spike Milligan

Ⓢ *Did he get the letter?*
Ⓢ *Wrote again Jan 6th*

———

9 Orme Court,
LONDON. .. 2.

6th January, 1970

President Richard M. Nixon,
White House Office,
1600 Pennsylvania Avenue N.W.,
Washington D.C.20500.
U.S.A.

Dear Mr. President,

I know you are a busy man; I assure you I work as many hours myself, but I would like a reply to my letter of the 17th September, 1969.

Respectfully,

Spike Milligan.

He's AN
ARSEHOLE.

———

Mrs Molly Ross
Birkenhead

9 April 1970

Dear Mrs Ross,

Thank you for your letter of Easter Sunday '70.

I will tell you why the hell I am worried about Wildlife; it's very simple. It's nearly all gone. If that isn't a priority need, then I don't know what is. Second thing is, the animals have no chance in newspaper appeals, no political party, nobody to take photographs of nuns holding them in their arms trying to save them. In other words, only the conscience married to intellect can ever do anything for them. Now, there is absolutely no shortage of human beings. They have satiated themselves to the extent where they are now turning out unwanted human beings by the thousand. This is the direct result of man himself. The destruction of the animal kingdom is also the work of man. So look at it through the cold eye of logic. One can immediately see where the priority is at its most urgent. This does not mean that I ignore my fellow man, I also work for human charities as well. I realise the pitiful agony of children born to a life of not being wanted, and they are never long out of my thoughts. Bearing their suffering in mind along with the fact that my fellow men are so debased as to give birth to children without any thought of whether they can provide for them or not. I joined the Family Planning International because that is where the heart of the problem is. Needless to say I am as distressed about the condition of children as you are, but I am also distressed about the extermination of animals.

Your description of where the children sleep 150 at a time is of course terrible, but I also witnessed in Nairobi last week, a baby chimpanzee with a broken leg in a tiny box, lying in its own excreta, which is also not very nice.

I will be trying to gather some money together for Mother Provincial, Loreto House, 7 Middleton Row, Calcutta.

I am also sending your letter to Oxfam who have thousands of bloody pounds especially for this purpose. Why aren't they sending any of it to these children? Have you approached them?

Anyhow, I will try.

Yours sincerely,
Spike Milligan

———◆———

The Editor
The Listener

25 June 1973

Dear Sir,

On Saturday 26th May (BBC 2) I watched an 'educational' programme. A man, with knife and scissors, stood over an anaesthetized white rabbit, slit it open, cut away with scissors, and removed the rabbit's heart, the heart was kept beating on a machine; the vivisector's voice purred on softly, and, no matter *who* argues to the contrary, I realised that the man had absolutely *no* feeling of remorse or sadness as to the destruction of the animal. Bearing in mind, he no doubt *believes* his actions are in the interest of mankind, we saw, that by continual repetition of taking life, the experimenter himself was being modified and dehumanised in his attitude to the taking of life. I have often pondered how German vivisectors in 1939 (apparently 'normal' men, just like our friend with the rabbit), went from animals to experiments with live men, women and children, the answer is simple, by continued association with suffering, the experiment finally becomes more important than the live creature, experiments mean death for the animal and to those who kill them a gradual and pernicious erosion of compassion and morals.

Respectfully,
Spike Milligan

Don't knock me off
I'm trying to Save the
Whales
Spike Milligan

[Note Spike put on his car whilst demonstrating in Trafalgar Square. You know what? They didn't.]

———◆———

HRH The Prince Philip, Duke of Edinburgh
Buckingham Palace

28 June 1973

Dear 'Skipper',

Good to see your name added to the signatories on the ten year ban on whale killing. There should be no let up to this fight, I am delighted that the battle is still on.

    Race you to grandfather.

Love, light and peace,
Spike Milligan

———◆———

The Earl of Antrim KBE
The National Trust
London S W1

6 June 1974

Dear Lord Antrim,

May I draw your attention to Page 22 of the National Trust Summer Issue (No. 20), there was an advert for Kirinyaga Game Safaris, and this included hunting, and that means killing.

I am certain the National Trust does not wish to advertise this sort of thing, and I wonder if you might terminate publishing it in any future issues.

The fight for conservation in my own area (Barnet) goes on a pace, my own Society (Finchley Society) after three years have only managed to save four buildings, but we have had success with tree planting and having preservation orders put on trees, so our gains in relationship to our efforts are by and large very small, but we continue to fight, and shall continue to fight.

My warm regards to you and all at the National Trust, without it I fear we would be ringed by filling stations and Tesco Supermarkets.

Love, light and peace,
Spike Milligan

THREE COUNTIES CAT SOCIETY

4th. June, 1974.

T.E.Cox, Esq.,
Animal Vigilantes,
High Street,
Fordingbridge.

Dear Mr. Cox,

      I have been instructed by my committee to write to you to say how very distressed we were to hear your President, Spike Milligan, say on the radio this week, that he kept an air gun to shoot at cats coming into his garden to hunt birds. As cats are natural predators, such behaviour, although regretable to bird lovers, must be accepted as a natural function.

      Mr. Milligan's practice of shooting at cats with an air-gun cannot be considered as anything but deplorably cruel in anyone, but in our view, such behaviour in a man holding the President's office in a movement devoted to the welfare of all animals, is quite beyond forgiveness and will, we fear, do your organisation considerable harm.

      In view of his actions, we are naturally, very glad that he did not accept our invitation to judge household pets at our show.

           Yours sincerely,

           Mary Wilson

           (Hon. Secretary).

ANIMALS' VIGILANTES

(AN EDUCATIONAL TRUST)

President : SPIKE MILLIGAN *United Against Cruelty To Animals*

Founder Chairman
TED COX, M.J.I.

TEC/LM

12th June 1974

Spike Milligan Esq.
9, Orme Court,
London. W.2.

Dear Spike,

    We have had a number of supporters resign after the statement you were alleged to have made on "World at One".

    I did not hear the programme and when the first letters arrived I replied saying this was a humorous remark made with no meaning. Various newspapers give varying reports but it is having a serious effect on our members. Can you please let me know what I should reply as I have in all cases made it very clear what you have done for the Cause and for the animal world.

    A copy of a letter from the Three Counties Cat Society is enclosed.

       Sincerely,

       Ted

(CONTRA)ICTED YOURSELF PUT

Ted Cox,

This letter will be a letter w ich you can photostat or copy and send to all these people who are "outraged by my cruelty towards cats".

It is very interesting that nobody seems at all concerned about the boy I shot, everybody said "good you should have shot him", but shoot a cat and the world is up in arms.

Now then, I am a man who is concerned with the whole spectrum of life and the sanctity of it, and believe it or not last month, I was outraged at the treatment given to an earthworm on the Open University Programme and as a result of it I wrote to Sir Charles Curran and the R.S.P.C.A. In the same week I was presenting a petition for the conservation of the largest living creature on earth, the whale, to the Jap. Embassy and the Russian Emb. So, no matter what these people think or say as the result of a report in a newspaper, they cannot take away from me the fact that I work on a greater scale of conservation than most of the people who are indicted me me over pussy cats. concerned with pussy cats alive.
They I have always been highly suspect of people who have only a one animal interest, these are usually the "Pussy Cat people" or the "poor little doggie people", and in the main I find they are psychologically unbalanced, and who have very little concern for any other living creatures, except the ones they worship, and rather like those people who belong to the RSPCA and hunt stags and foxes to death. I notice that the Three Counties Cat Society are outraged by the fact I keep an airgun to shoot at cats who come into the garden to hunt birds.

First, let me tell you that I have two cats of my own, both of whom love me and are well feed and are well treated, we also have a rabbit, a guinea pig and a goldfish I myself put up lots of nesting boxes in my garden; now, when I see a well fed sleek cat about to kill the fledglings or raid the nests and I am unable to get there physically to stop their death I take the action of shooting at the cat with a air pellet. This does no more than sting the cat and it saves the lives of helpless fledglings.

This act of mine is considered cruel, apparently I should stand by an and let the cat destroy the fledglings and then the pussy cat people would be perfectly happy - well I'm afraid I cannot reduce myself to that miniscule method of thinking. They say the cats are natural predators, and although regrettable to bird lovers must be, the cats accepted as a natural function, Well, if they believe in natural function its instinct, and my natural function and instinct is was to save the birds, and if the cat has the right to exercise that instinct, likewise I have the right to exercise mine, in this case to protect the birds fledgelings.

SHOOT CATS

- 2 -

✱ *NOT SHOT ONE*

Now, ~~todate~~ I have ~~not done this to any cats,~~ *never shot a cat* as I have managed
to shoo them away before they have destroyed the birds, but
its on the cards, that if I can't get to the cat in time I will
use the air rifle, which will save the lives of birds, and will
do no more than sting the cat. ~~Likewise if people~~ *In conclusion if*
people are going to sit in judgement of other people by what they read
in newsapapers, there is no hope for any of us.

I hope this letter has made clear my feelings and if the Animal
Vigilantes decide as a result of this letter that I am a not
fit person to be the President I am perfectly willing to
resign.   But, nevertheless, I will still go on what I believe
to be right because that is all I ever can do.

~~P.S.~~ I would like to add that I am also a vegetarian as a protest
against the outrageous factory farming, and likewise I do not use
products made of leather, and I make sure that the cat food my cats
eat are not from animals ~~in~~ under threat of extinction like
kangaroo meat.   I wonder if any of the pussy cat people are doing
as much.

'As ever
Spike Milligan

———————•———————

J. O. Petterrson Esq.
National Environment Protection Board
Sweden

18 September 1975

Dear Sir,

I wonder if you can give me any information regarding the native
Swedish wolf. I believe the numbers are down to about one
dozen. Is your Government making any special provisions to see
these animals don't become extinct.

If so, can you tell me what they are.

Sincerely,
Spike Milligan
Member of the World Wildlife Committee

———•———

Elton John Esq.

1 May 1981

Dear Elton,

It has come to my ears that you think I am displeased with you. Well, it's all very confusing. I wrote around to a few of the pop luminaries trying to get £1,500 to save elephant families from being slaughtered, and transported to a game reserve where they would survive; and I wrote to you, the letter was sent to your address in Los Angeles, I got it from your London office as you were there at the time, the address I sent it to was – c/o. Rocket Records, 211 Beverley Drive, Suite 205, Los Angeles, 90212.

(a) I never received a reply from you, and (b) I never received a reply from whoever received the letter. If a creep who opened the letter didn't tell you she/he/it/shithead is responsible for my feelings towards you, because the least I expect of anybody is a reply to a letter. It's like when you turn a tap on you expect water. If you received my letter personally and didn't reply then my opinion of you is valid, but I have heard from Joan Thirkettle of ITN News that you said you never received a letter. This message was passed on to me by my Manager, Norma Farnes – let's all four, take our clothes off, join hands and play ring-a-ring-a nettles.

So, over to you to tell me where the truth lies. Personally I would much prefer you had sent £14,000 to Save the Elephant, and let somebody else pay £13,000 to buy the scripts. That way the world, for my money, would be better off.

However, it's not too late to send me £1,500 to save an elephant, you can name the elephant whatever you choose.

I think we should call it after the secretary who never sent you my letter, then you can buy a female elephant, and I will buy a male elephant and call it Hitler, and in the mating season we can go and watch Hitler fucking your secretary.

Apart from that all is well.

Love, light and peace,
Spike Milligan

WATFORD
ASSOCIATION FOOTBALL CLUB LTD
DIVISION III CHAMPIONS 1968/69
Members of the Football League   The Mid-week Football League

Chairman E H John
Manager G Taylor
General Manager/Secretary R E Rollitt, FAAI

REGISTERED OFFICE AND GROUND
VICARAGE ROAD WATFORD WD1 8ER
Telephone Watford 21759/24729
Registered Number 104194 ENGLAND

May 12th 1981.

Dear Spike

Thanks for your letter. I'm completely unaware of the letter you sent me regarding saving elephants – and nobody connected with my office ever passed it on. Heads will role! To put matters right I am sending you a cheque and would like to name the elephant Betty (after my personal assistant) and if someone else could buy one called Nick Nolte we can watch Nick Nolte fuck Betty (she's mad about him).

Can I say that already (my life). He scripts have given cause for much hilarity. Unfortunately, the writers of 'Mrs Dale's Diary', 'Monty Python' and 'Emergency Ward 10', have been inundating me with scripts!!

WATFORD
ASSOCIATION FOOTBALL CLUB LTD
DIVISION III CHAMPIONS 1968/69
Members of the Football League   The Mid-week Football League

Chairman E H John
Manager G Taylor
General Manager/Secretary R E Rollitt, FAAI

REGISTERED OFFICE AND GROUND
VICARAGE ROAD WATFORD WD1 8ER
Telephone Watford 21759/24729
Registered Number 104194 ENGLAND

Also, if the BBC ever let you loose on the public again with Q6 and I'm not touring or signing footballers - would love to do something with you - I'll rephrase that - would love to do the show.

Glad to see you are well - saw you on that terrible Wogan show. I'm not going to buy a wig - just a nice set of Lady Di and HRH dinner plates.

Love

Elton.

The Right Honourable Tony Blair MP
Prime Minister
10 Downing Street

6 *March 1998*

Dear Prime Minister,

Please could you do something about terminating these horrible mink fur farms as the animals live in the most appalling conditions. If you have any Christian feeling, would you please try to put an end to this.

Sincerely,
Spike Milligan

P. S. I'm a Catholic, come and join us.

8

Here is the Dilemma

The Editor
Daily Express

16 July 1970

Dear Sir,

Recently in one of your leaders you criticised Mr Anthony Greenwood as having failed as Labour's Housing Minister.

I can only say that in all my dealings with him regarding preservation of buildings, he answered all the letters, went to great lengths to help with information, he also showed great concern when the subject of preservation arose, and for my money he has been one of the best Housing Ministers that has been my good fortune to deal with.

When it comes to Housing, can you name a Housing Minister whose housing programme ever caught up with the birth rate, and no Minister ever will, until the Ministry of Depopulation is set up.

Sincerely,
Spike Milligan

P. S. Isn't the weather marvellous.

—•—

World Wildlife News

12 August 1970

Dear Sirs,

In your summer issue of the World Wildlife News, you ask the question regarding Farming and Wildlife.

There is only one answer, and always has been one answer, and that is population control. Nobody can compromise with ever expanding population, to try and compromise with that is sheer madness, and at the moment madness is at the helm.

We are tearing down hedges and trees in England to provide food, OK go on tearing down the hedges and the trees and we eventually arrive at a treeless and hedgeless England, because every acre has to be cut down for the ever increasing mouths of population.

Now, what happens after that. We will start, I presume drying out the oceans and the seas and reclaiming lands (as they are in Holland). You can go on and on like this, but it shows only too clearly that world leaders haven't got a clue as to how to treat this urgent problem.

If we are to save what is left of the earth surfaces being stripped of all wild vegetation *there must be a crash birth control programme at once.*

So the answer to the question 'Where can we compromise?', is WE DON'T.

Love, light and peace,
Spike Milligan

The Editor
The Times

30 November 1970

Sir,

The Pope's visit to the poor family in Tondo.

Were it not for his integrity (and this is unquestionable) the situation was like a very sick joke.

I was sorry for him, I was sorry for the Mother and Father, but most of all I was sorry for the eight children born unnecessarily so into a life of poverty.

If ever there was clear evidence supporting Family Planning this was the occasion.

I hope the Holy Father will reflect on it.

Yours etc.
Spike Milligan

Messrs. Jack Hoy & S. Mitchell
Issue
(Furtherwick Park School Newspaper)

10 January 1972

Dear Lads,

Basically, here is the dilemma:

> COPULATION EQUALS POPULATION
> EQUALS POLLUTION.
> ANSWER: BIRTH CONTROL.

Sincerely,
Spike Milligan

———◆———

The Editor
The Guardian

20 January 1976

Dear Sir,

Re the recent brou ha-ha over immigration statistics, here is another set of confusing statistics. I have written to the Prime Minister saying in view of the population explosion the appointment of a Minister of Population is more than pressing. In a reply from 10 Downing Street it was quoted that Lord Shepherd pointed out 'that the birth rate in this country has been falling for the past eight years and the latest figures show virtually no increase in population'. Then HM Stationery Office publishes a paper, Population Projection No. 4 which says: 'There are 56 million people in the U. K. this is expected to increase to

59.2 million by the year 2,000.' Like Alice said 'It's very confusing';
the trouble is somebody somewhere is getting paid to confuse us.

Respectfully,
Spike Milligan

*[Was he even right and it still goes on. For all the talk nothing has changed
in thirty-seven years but the figures, and they are increased every year.]*

———•———

Gurth Hoyer Miller Esq.
OXFAM

12 November 1976

Dear Gurth Hoyer Miller (though I would never know from your
signature, I had to refer to the printed name at the bottom of the
paper – oh! your poor bank manager).

Of course I would like to be a Vice President, but I must make it
clear that in my past dealings with Oxfam, and this goes back
about 20 years, when I openly came out against Oxfam who
refused to become involved in population control, I still put this
at the top of my agenda, because basically our humanitarian
urges are to feed the starving, help the sick and the suffering, but
that will only help ameliorate our own feelings, it will never solve
the problem. The problem is a statistical one, that is numbers. We
have to reduce them at all costs or we shall *all* perish.

'You have got to be cruel to be kind', is an old adage, but in the
light of population it takes on a new meaning. You are no doubt
aware of India's enforcement of sterilisation for all people who
have two children. I myself don't like the idea of it, but then that
is my humanitarian feelings being outraged, and I realise that the
idea is basically sound.

Having said all this, just to let you know 'where I'm at' regarding attitudes to charities.

Now, of course as Oxfam has contributed part of their funds to population control, I am happy to say I would like to be a Vice President.

Love, light and peace,
Spike Milligan

David Shannon Esq.
HONEY

30 June 1983

Dear David,

Question to Spike Milligan.

    Q) What would you do, if you ruled the world.

    A) Sell it.

If you want to elucidate on this, the most important thing I would do would be to snip off the testicles of every man who had more than two children, and set up a Parliament for the Rights of the Unborn Child to have civilised parents. Thirdly, I would re-wallpaper Dennis Thatcher.

Sincerely,
Spike Milligan

[Milligan has just lost his testicles or he forgot he had four children. When I reminded him of this fact he used to say 'Well you haven't got any so you can have two of mine'.]

The Letters Editor
Daily Telegraph
FAX
Pages 1/1

Sir,

I was pretty shocked by the publication of a letter from Robert Whelan regarding the article on World Population (July 11th). This man, Robert Whelan, is head of a quango who heads people of like mind that is, there is no problem with over-population all his letter promoted was a bigger population. I have tried repeatedly to find out who finances his organisation which is Committee of Population and (wait for it) the Economy. He will only say 'we are privately financed'. I suspect the private money comes from large firms that can only increase revenue by having an increased population. This man is an environmental idiot.

Sincerely,
Spike Milligan

———◆———

Daily Telegraph
Letters Page
FAX
1 page only

Sir,

Neville Wheelan believes that the Cairo conference on world population is an effort by western powers for selfish reasons to reduce world population. Is it selfish to try and make more room on this planet? It is not, as he says, a massive programme on contraception. It is to *advise* people having children beyond their means to curtail the number of children. He says 'anyone with an ounce of common sense can grasp that a large population means greater wealth'. The very city that the conference is being held has a population of 66 millions and desperately poor – how many millions more do they need to become rich?

If numbers of population relate to wealth how is it that the richest country in the world has 6 millions – Switzerland with earning per capita 27.5 hundred whereas Japan with a population of 123 millions has a earning per capita of 21.00 hundred. How can he explain the disparity? Can you tell me why the figure with such a huge population is not 50/100 times more than of Switzerland?

Finally Mr Wheelan we live on a finite world when he fills it up, what then?

Spike Milligan

Letters Editor
Daily Telegraph

12 July 1994

Sir,

I am afraid predictions of world population declining to the level of the 1980s (11 July) is really not on.

I see that Mr Johnston is going to distribute family planning to 10 million couples or people – this is a drop in the ocean. The population stands now between six and seven billion, and he quotes the decline of 2.71 million in the years 2010. Well, I have a report from the Office of Population Censuses saying that our present population is 56 millions, and is going to increase in the year 2000 by 5.9 millions, it doesn't seem to auger very good for the predictions of depopulation. When you come to think of it China with their one child policy put on a population growth of 13 millions a year. The basic problem is not a matter of how much family planning is given, its the most powerful biological urge in the world is a woman who wants a child, and she will go ahead and have one and she may want another and another and she will ignore any family planning.

No, to stop world population we need a world moratorium on births for five years.

Sincerely,
Spike Milligan

—•—

The Daily Mail

20 December 1994

Sir,

The discovery by the boffins that new roads would only encourage more traffic – why don't they look beyond that and see a burgeoning population will buy more and more cars and so it is no good those people with large families complaining about traffic going through their villages and towns when they have, possibly like I have, four children each with a motor car.

Sincerely,
Spike Milligan

—•—

Alexander
c/o Jonathan Porrit
Gloucestershire

20 December 1994

Dear Alexander,

Here is my very brief idea of the future.

In the future due to over population the world will be crowded to bursting point. While animals will have been exterminated by human pressure the country will be one mass of motorways and millions of cars sending out fumes in the atmosphere.

That is my opinion of the future; sorry it is so glum but I am facing up to the truth, even as I speak millions are being born.

Sincerely,
Spike Milligan

PART THREE
Writing It Off

9

Internal Mail

The Fucking Grass

Norma —

13 July 5.30. Ive just spoke
to Nanna — a boy from Gentle
Ghost arrived yesterday — he
worked on the Lawn for 2.
hours — ~~then~~ ~~was~~ he
didn't finish the Job —
the edges need cutting with
shears — The ~~Rotor Scythe~~
~~John~~ He then asked Nanna
for £2.50 — She paid —
This is getting to be a full time
Job for me. WILL YOU GET SOMEBODY
ANY BODY TO FINISH THE
FUCKING JOB FROM START TO
FINISH — AND THEY DONT
GET PAID UNTIL BOTH

LAWNS ARE CUT and
trimmed — and all grass
cuttings dumped in the
Stream

PLEASE IF I
COME BACK AND
NOTHING HAS HAPPENED
Its the end
        Love
        Spel

The Jcoder with the Rotary
Sythe <u>hasn't appeared</u>

Dear Norma

Part III week 4 of
how to buy a pen.
This time please give me
where they sell them.
The address and phone
number and I'll do it
myself

Love
Speh

April 1983　　65TH BIRTHDAY
AUSTRALIAN TOUR.

BIRTHDAY CARDS ONLY.

A) IF I'D SENT THEM ON: "WASTING
FUCKING MONEY ON POSTAGE"

B) IF I'D NOT KEPT THEM "WHAT ~~YOU~~
DO YOU MEAN I WANTED THE CARDS
FROM MY FANS"

C) I DID KEEP THEM SO: "WHAT DID
YOU KEEP THESE FOR, MY FUCKING
BIRTHDAY WAS 2 MONTHS AGO"

PLEASE TICK.　ERIC SYKES
SAID
/
WHERE APPLICABLE

[A note from me when he was on tour in Australia. Eric said, 'Oh Norma you're getting like him.']

[Spike responds to one of my notes to him . . .]

I came to the office but you had left for Brideshead — so I couldn't follow up the BOOKMAN issue. Pauline Sandimore <u>has</u> the Newspaper rights but says she will not exercise them. I <u>know</u> you dont believe. <u>Me</u> — ? I dont give a fuck any more. — now read one......

5/7/85

<u>TIM SLESSOR</u> . <u>BBC</u>. AUSTRALIAN

<u>DOCUMENTARY</u> — is BACK FROM

WONDERS !!!!!

AUSTRALIA: YOUR DIRECTOR FOR THE

SHOW, WILL BE <u>ANDY STEVENSON</u>.

at last! a name!

I'VE TOLD HIM ITS NOT POSSIBLE

never never her very

TO SPEAK TO YOU DURING DAY, AND

I do everything on the news never

ANDY HAS GOT YOUR HOME NUMBER

whats wrong with the telephone?

HE'LL RING YOU THIS EVENING JUST

TO MAKE CONTACT. The excitement.

2·30 on 25¹²

<u>26TH JULY</u>: MY DIARY IS CLEAR

CAN TIM AND ANDY COME TO

MONKENHURST ON THAT DAY FOR

A TALK ON YOUR IDEAS YOU

SUBMITTED — JUST TO ENLARGE ON THEM.

we already agreed this dear

MORE.

S. JORGE (Madeira)
Restaurante CABANA
CABANA restaurant
Restaurant CABANA

Hello Norma + Tanis -
I'm the youngest man on
the ship. Bent cripples
staggering everywhere -
7 Burials a day at sea -
Food 7/10 Cabins 6/10 -
www OK - Enjoying the
break. Now what?
Love Spike +

N Farnes. Tanis Davis

Bayswater
London W2
ENGLAND

[I had said, 'Go on a cruise, it will do you good. You need the rest.' – Hence 'Now what?']

Oct 27.

Hello Miss North Country
at 1949.
POST CARD
Guess what? they put me up
in a noisy motel - lonely.
however. have now god
a house in the bush.
lonely, saw a wallaby
on the lawn this morning)
All to order. Weather
lovely. Day off today -
alone - lots of showers -
classics on ABC Radio -
writing Vol III warmemoirs
Love Spike

Norma 'I'll never get married
again' Farnes

Bayswater
London
W2
UK

[My perpetual question to him was 'Are you getting on with the book?'
When I knew he wasn't. Holiday PC to ease my mind.]

OLD MELBOURNE GAOL
This bluestone Gaol complex was
built 1841 – 62. Since then it has
sheltered more than 50,000 pris-
oners.
Model of Harry Power, the
bushranger.
NATIONAL TRUST OF
AUSTRALIA (VICTORIA)
Open for public inspection

NU-COLOR-VUE

NAT 6
NCV 2784

POST CARD

Dear Norma Tanis –
Melbourne went well –
back into the suitcase
and onto Tasmania –
I'm pressing on writing to
finish the book of
numerous poems – love to
all – Love Spels

Can u pass
enclosed PC to
Mike Haynes. Ta.

[Same sentiments. Still trying to ease my mind – different book.]

I found quite Safari
Ranch. Living in Rondavels
Zebra - Deer - Geese
Peacocks - roam the grounds.
Food 7/10 Wine 19/10 But
Quiet. Show going very well.
Warm days. Cold nights -
by day I'm writing Vol V
of War Memoirs - alas I don't
have the mass of ref books I
need. Love to Tann

Mrs N Farnes

Bayswater
London
W 2
England

[He's still at it. Different book but now an excuse.]

WINSOR·BECK
P·U·B·L·I·C R·E·L·A·T·I·O·N·S

Norman Farnes
9 Orme Court
London W2

21 April 1988

Dear Ms Farnes

Re: Premiere of "Jane & The Lost City"

We are currently arranging the premiere of Jasper Carrott's new
movie "Jane & The Lost City", the film version of the adventures
of the Daily Mirror's most famous strip cartoon "Jane".

The film will be having a Charity Royal Premiere on May 11 at the
Odeon Marble Arch, with Prince Edward as guest of honour and
there will be a party at the Dorchester Hotel afterwards.

Through your goodself we would like to extend an invitation to
Spike Milligan to be our guest on the evening.

Please call me if he would like to attend and I will arrange to
get the tickets to him.

Yours sincerely,

Geri Winsor

Geri Winsor
Director

Sholagh

*Over to you. Let
me know if ya
want to go.*

Send tickets but

WHAT BLOODY TIME

You

439. 2244

YOU ARE TOO BLOODY LATE

RECEIVED 16/5

[Spike, oh dear. Petty, would you say? Note the incorrect spelling of his name.]

28 November 1988

Dear Spike

Many thanks for your letter of 23 November, to a Mr Allen Brook; I am answering the letter on his behalf.

I'm afraid your friend at Frankfurt didn't investigate closely enough; we certainly did have a copy of McGONAGALL on the stand - possibly on the last day it got stolen by the German hordes who stripped the stands of all our books.

I was delighted to see THE LOONEY at No.6 this Sunday; ✻ what are the plans for your literary outpourings next year? ✻

All the best

Yours   ✻ Clerkecy - letter writing -

Alan Brooke

Norma, Secretaries! - are there any professional ones? They are ruining my life -

2 Dec 1988

Dear Alan,

I see you are annoyed at your
name being spelt 'Allen Brook –
what can one do this is not my
Country – the secretaries are English –
they are educated by English teachers
under an English system of education
owing to pressure of work I have
to dictate my letters over the phone
and have them pp signed by (and)
posted by them – I don't see the
letter, I spell as many words as
I can for the ignorant bastards –
alas this time the ignorant bastard

spell you name wrong - in future
I will spell you name out to
them, I just want you to know
it was not my fault, but the
English education system. I'm
glad you had _one_ of my books
on display. my friend was looking
for a display of them.

                    Yours .
                    Spike

PS note I have dispensed with a
   typist
          S

[Today we hate the English. Tomorrow? Anybody's guess. Depends on who is going to upset him.]

Telemessage

KEA3273 LLW8674 PBA0002 P10 5098LOND   07 DEC 1988/1031

---

07 December 1988

TELEMESSAGE
NORMA FARNES
9 ORME COURT
BAYSWATER
LONDON W2

> IT'S NOW 10.30 AND NEITHER YOU NOR DIANNA ARE IN THE OFFICE. IN
> FUTURE COULD BOTH OF YOU ARRANGE TO INFORM EACH OTHER AND IN TURN
> INFORM ME. JUST PICK UP THE PHONE AND CALL ME.
>   SPIKE.

[Oh. What a Prickly Pear. I'm not there when he needed me – Diddums!!!]

Telemessage®

KEA0686 LLV8507 PAI0007 P08 1544LOND   23 MAY 1990/1049

9 Orme Court
Bayswater
London W2 4RL

23 May 1990

TELEMESSAGE
NORMA FARNES
9 ORME COURT
BAYSWATER
LONDON W2 4RL

> PLEASE TELL ME WHEN YOU ARE ALL NOT GOING TO BE IN.

> SPIKE.

To Norma Farnes (if shes in)
9 Orme Court.
Bayswater
London
W2

10

The Rise and Fall of Oblomov

Bernard Miles Esq.
Mermaid Theatre
London EC4

6 November 1964

Thank you for your letter and the cuttings.

I am sorry you couldn't take 'Oblomov' as well. I think you have turned down a money spinner. It makes no difference to me whether the play goes on or not, as I have got lots of other work, but it is a pity to see a genuine success without a home to go to.
    Anyhow regards to all.

[Oblomov had been performed out of London prior to this letter . . .]

———— •◆• ————

Charles Marowitz Esq.
London NW1

6 November 1964

I have just had brought to my notice a criticism of 'Oblomov' in 'Encore'. Christ!. I can never live up to it, but nevertheless thanks for a shot of literary adrenalin.

Regards,
Spike Milligan

———— •◆• ————

Sunday 1 November 1964

Dear Mulligan,

On Thursday evening I left the New Lyric filled with strong tea
and chagrin. That doesnt sound right . . . What would a theatre
look like if filled up to slopping over with strong tea and chagrin?
Obviously it must have been me was filled with the tea and chag.
And I sat down and wrote you an kindly harsh note. Which I've
lost. You apologized for the fact that someone had been paid to
write or lets say wrote some of those mouldering fustian lines
you had to speak.

I am puzzled. Why didnt you rewrite the play yourself after the
first rehearsal, after the first reading?

Why didnt you throw the whole rag bag away and you and
Owen sit on the bed and make jokes?

It didnt need the Bed Sitting Room to prove that you knew
better. You know better. Excepting that you are being
blackmailed. That must be the explanation.

As an Irishman why dont you spell your name properly?

As an Irishman I know how to spell *my* name properly.

I'm in love with a girl with a closed mind of her own. What
shall I do?

Here's a book in which if you are lucky you may find a few
jokes to see you through till Saturday.

Yours,
Ernest Gebler

P. S. Do you want to buy in to buying the lower half of
        County Cork?

Ernest Gebler Esq.
London SW20

6 *November 1964*

Dear Ernest Gebler,

Thank you for your 'out of the blue' letter.

Answering your queries. I did not re-write the play because it would have taken me three months to do this. I did not re-write the play after the first rehearsal because the cast seemed oblivious as to the rubbish they were reading and who am I an Irishman to put the English on the right track? It is my duty to go down with the ship full of the English. It is worth one Irishman dying to enjoy that pleasure. Having let the ship sink I have now salvaged the whole thing on my own by ad libing all the way through, proving conclusively that they were wrong, blind and stupid.

I cannot sit on the bed and tell jokes with Bill Owen, because Bill Owen cannot crack jokes. He is a nice man but terribly pedantic and therefore unfunny.

The overall explanation to the play's disaster lies in the fact that there are few people in the theatre who can look at the written word and imagine whether it is good or not.

As to my not spelling my name properly, may I inform you that your version, i.e. Mulligan is also wrong. If you must know the correct word is O'Malagáin. Sometimes attenuated to O'Maoileagáin. How is that for shooting you down in flames?

Yes, I want to buy the lower half of County Cork. Can you quote me a price.

Spike Milligan

Captain L. A. Milligan MSM, RNA, Rt'd
New South Wales
Australia

18 November 1964

Dear Dad,

Your letter of 11th November to hand.

I am glad you enjoyed the 'Encore' article. I found it a bit over-powering, I don't think any human being in the world should get too much praise because after all it is our maker who gave us the talent, and not us who created it. You will be glad to hear that the play 'Oblomov' ran successfully for five weeks at the Lyric, Hammersmith despite a justifiable panning by the critics, and now we are transferring to the Comedy Theatre, London. If it runs successfully, there, I might have to postpone bringing 'The Bed Sitting Room' to Australia, because naturally it is financially more beneficial to play in London. However, if it runs a long time I will be able to afford to fly to Australia without the necessity of having to put on a play.

I am glad you have settled down again. I must say I get a great yearning whenever I think of Woy-Woy and those glorious sunny mornings, which just would not let you stay in bed, and the Pelican flying around over the water and the unforgettable sight of Dolphin playing as they went out towards Gosford.

I will buy the Charlie Chaplin book. I did write to him in Switzerland sending him a copy of my book and offering him one of the bronze handles which came off the old Metropole Variety Theatre bar door, but he did not bother to answer the letter, so he got one point in my estimation.

I hope Mum is keeping well. I had a letter from Desmond in which he told me about the Clun's marriage breaking up and Desmond having to give food and shelter to Mrs Clun. It seems that the Milligans are eternally cursed with women trouble. If I were born again I should like to be a tree, and even this someone would come along and chop me down.

Harry Edgington and his family are coming back. He wrote to me saying that he felt his family held him somewhat responsible for the decline of their fortunes, which is the way modern families treat the head of the household.

I didn't read the first half of your book as it came in and went out the same day. Don't be too disappointed if they send it back because that is what usually happens. It happened to me with 'Puckoon'. It was thrown back by three publishers, all of whom must have cursed themselves when it became a best seller.

I must dash now. I will write again soon.

Your loving son,
Terry

———◆———

Captain & Mrs L. A. Milligan
New South Wales
Australia

11 December 1964

Dear Dad,

This is a letter just to explain how my rather bumpy career is shaping. The play 'Oblomov' opened at the Lyric, Hammersmith to bad notices, but sympathetic in general to me. The trouble was I took the part of 'Oblomov' because at the time I had no other work. I knew it was a busy play but I had to sacrifice my beliefs for bread and butter. I did everything that the producers, managers and great actors told me to do. The result, was disastrous but it was no surprise to me and I knew that the play would get a slating. However, I decided to do something about it, in fact I was the ONLY person who could do anything about it, so I started to ad lib my way through the show and bit by bit made it into an extremely funny show. The result was during the five weeks we were at the Lyric, Hammersmith we broke the box office record twice. It was then transferred to the West End to the Comedy Theatre, where it opened to rave notices, from the very critics who had decried it on the original opening night. In the first week we have broken the box office record for Saturdays, and the box office record for every other day of the week. I cant really believe it but there it is, it is actually happening.

I suppose at the age of 47 I can say that success did not come until I was nearly 50, which is a long time. However, it is happening and there seems no let up in the bookings. The only trouble is I fear that this unexpected success will stop me going to Australia next March in 'The Bed Sitting Room'. Nevertheless, I will be coming to Australia at the very first opportunity because I like it out there. In fact, if I had enough money I would settle out there permanently, which of course is still more than a possibility.

Paddy is sending you all the cuttings, as she wanted to be the person who told you. I am just sending this letter in case the cuttings go astray. I have received your Christmas card. All the children and Paddy are well. I fluctuate between being well and unwell according to how people treat me. Of course, what has made a big difference to me is this play because I had saved up a thousand pounds and hoped to buy a piece of ground in the country and try to build a home on it for myself, but when I saw the possibility of 'Oblomov' being a success I put that thousand pounds into the play, and I am keeping my fingers crossed that the play will run long enough for the thousand pounds to make a profit.

Well that is all the news for now. I will try to telephone you during the next fortnight. God bless you all.

As ever,
Your loving son,
Terry

Michael White Esq.
London SW1

12 April 1965

Dear Michael,

I am writing you this letter in the light of having discovered that Ricardo Arragno has in fact been given 5% as the 'author' of the show. It means in fact that I have been writing, and by writing that I think of an idea, because I don't write it down, nevertheless it has the same significance and comes under the heading of material.

Up to date I have done this for nothing, but I think that I should be entitled to something for the efforts. I certainly am not being greedy, and to have written a flop, and to get 5% of it thereafter, mainly because I had, let's face it, saved the play because of my training as a writer, and it is on this basis that I think I should in future get a percentage.

I at least do not want to go on keeping the play alive for free, because basically that is what I have been doing for the last six months, and if Mr Arragno wishes to continue with the same financial arrangements, whereas he may be satisfied I am not. Like all of us I am in this for the money, and I do not intend to go on making money for everybody when the actual provider of the success, namely the material I have invented, is the basis of the financial success of the play.

I do hope you understand, I do not know of many people who would write new material for six months for nothing, so you can see I am not greedy, I just want a fair cut for the effort I have put into the play. I do hope you understand and we can still continue our amicable relationship.

Regards as ever,
Spike Milligan

MEMO PAD

FROM ___David Conyers___   Date ___24th March 1966___

SUBJECT ___JEPPE OF THE MOUNTAIN___

TO _____Spike Milligan_____

Spike

●
            Herewith a copy of a letter from Peter
         Rawley which is self-explanatory together
         with the script to which his letter refers.

Do you still~~, urg~~ want to
read this? I will give
it a preliminary read; if you ~~let~~

●   David/ there is no point in
    me reading it. I am, ~~for financial~~
    reasons condemed to serve
    a life sentence in Oblimor until
    my ~~financial~~ life is sorted out.
    and that will be at least
    another year away. S

Milligan to Quit 'Oblomov,' He Sez During the Show

London, April 12.

[Son of Oblomov *was a huge hit at the* Comedy Theatre, *breaking all box office records. But then, suddenly, after the curtain had risen on one performance, Spike called a press conference and invited journalists in the audience up onto the stage to announce he was quitting the show.*

To a stunned audience he said, 'You must be puzzled. You see it was raining when I arrived at the theatre and I couldn't talk to these gentlemen then, so I've invited them on stage to talk now.'

For me, vintage Milligan.]

11

Publish and Be Damned

Dear Norma,

Quick note.

Suggest to Michael Joseph - 2nd Vol be
called   Rommel. -   (war in
                  my part in   Africa
                  his downfall

Vol 3   Mussolini -   War In
                  my part in   Italy
                  his downfall

Vol 4   Maria Antonietta Pontani   Post war.
                  my part in her   Italy.
                  downfall   to de-mob
                                                demob

Still I'll in bed. But temperature subsiding. What bloody luck.
What a year! Sorry I've not not written and
and felt to Grotten. - I've had to cancel the Une
Show. but will do it when I'm better.

hope all is well.
                              Love
                              Spike

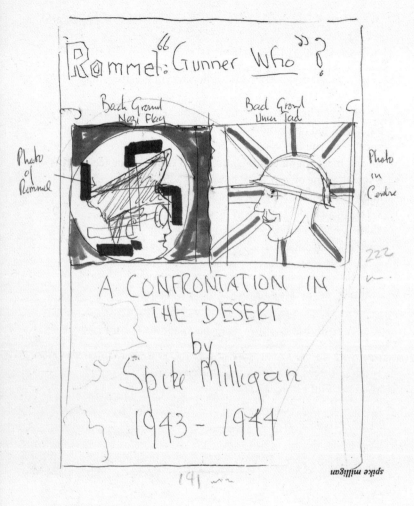

spike milligan

[Spike. Working well today.]

March 6th

Dear Spike Milligan,

May I be allowed to send you a little word of greeting and admiration?

When you have given as much of yourself as *you* have to the big B. P. – and other Publics abroad, you are so right to stop at once when you feel you must, and you are so courageous to do so, and to let your admiring public into your confidence . . . This is just the time of year to take some rest and *refreshment*, and I hope you do it thoroughly, for all our sakes'.

I have such pleasant memories of our meeting in Australia. There is heaps more work waiting which only you can do but you must take *in* sometimes instead of giving out all the time.

So I venture to send you my very best wishes for the right kind of rest, and great benefit therefrom.

Please do not think this letter needs an answer . . . I know so well what it is to feel overtired – but all will be well, and fresh strength will come, sooner than you imagine, in abundant measure.

Yours sincerely, with every possible good wish,
Margaret Rutherford

[What a wonderful letter to him.]

MILLIGAN CONFUSION.

Some confusion has arisen over the promotional activities, or not,
of Spike Milligan, following two seperate advertisements which
appeared in the Bookseller last week. The promotional plans
for Spike Milligan: A Biography by Pauline Scudamore, published
by Granada, will feature the author rather than Mr Milligan
himself.
Mr Milligan, however, will be busy promoting his own "WHERE
HAVE ALL THE BULLETS GONE" the fifth volume of his autobiography
to be published by Michael Joseph, in association with M. & J
Hobbs.

SPIKE THIS IS THE WORDING, AND RICHARD SHILLITO THE SOLICITOR,
STATES QUITE CATEGORICALLY, IT SAYS ABSOLUTELY NOTHING ABOUT
SERIALISATION RIGHTS, AND REFERS ONLY TO YOUR ACCOMPANING
HER ON PROMOTION.

I would like to talk to you while this
was fresh on my mind, but you had gone
North. Like wise to my horror I find a
GALLEY proof from Sedgewich + Jackson –
This is a fucking ~~house~~ nerve – one) you
never mentioned the word GALLEY PROOFS TO ME,
you only mentioned captions – which you said –
you death until – They want me to spend my
week end why they are all away – well
&m not doing it – this is the 2nd time
this has happened last time it was FLAWED
MASTERPIECES – on a Friday to be ready
monday – I DONT WANT ANY MORE
WEEK END CHORES – Like you I want a break –
so please remember –
Spike

PS Im suppoed to be learning my TV Script

Dick Douglas-Boyd Esq.
Michael Joseph Limited

2 December 1977

Dear Dick,

Thank you so much for the leatherbound copy of Puckoon. How did you know that the colour I hate most is purple – the divine inspirational.

If I can have a choice in future, can I have black, or brown – or red to go with my bank balance.

As ever,
Spike Milligan

———◆———

Michael Joseph Ltd
London WC1

6 December 1977

Dear Spike,

My favourite leather is black shiny. I am sorry that you don't like purple. It cost us a hell of a lot of money because the binding is made entirely of baboon bums and it is hard to find one large enough to fit round anything but a paperback.

Tell you what, if we have a good year next year you'll get black. If we're in the red you'll get red. O.K?

Yours,
Dick
Richard Douglas-Boyd

———◆———

Dick Douglas-Boyd Esq.

14 January 1978

Dear Dick,

Regarding being in the red or black – we are all going to be in the shit, so I suggest a brown cover.

As ever,
Spike Milligan

———————•———————

[Spike received a letter from Mrs M. H. Reith, Northview Junior Mixed School, saying that they had been examining their library books for any that contained anything racially or sexually offensive. Spike's children's book, Dip the Puppy, *contained a character called King Blackbottom, so she informed him they were recommending to the Director of Education that* Dip the Puppy *be excluded from all school and children's libraries in the Borough of Brent. Spike's reply:]*

Mrs M. H. Reith
London Borough of Brent Education Committee
Northview Junior Mixed & Infants School

3 June 1982

Dear Mrs Reith,

If you feel free to remove the book because of the mention of 'KING BLACKBOTTOM', I am a complete believer in freedom; but you don't sound as though you are enjoying it.

Love, light and peace,
Spike Milligan

P. S. Perhaps if I had put 'KING WHITEBOTTOM'.

———————•———————

[The offender.]

[This letter came out of the blue and he forgot to let me have a copy. Spike pretending to be a business man. It always ended in failure.]

Jack Hobbs Esq.
Richard Douglas-Boyd Esq.

1 September 1982

Dear Jack and Dick,

I would like to reassess my relationship with Jack Hobbs and Michael Joseph Limited. For instance, in the case of Sir Nobonk, I find the position with the financial distribution unjust to Carol Barker, in as much (a) it was her idea entirely. I wrote it without any consultation with Jack Hobbs, and Carol Barker was the one that was instrumental in getting the book together and all in all I think she should have come in for a fair share of the royalties.

I also understand, which I did not know, that Jack puts up half the money for my books. I would like this arrangement to come to an end as from this letter. I would like to negotiate new terms.

Sincerely,
Spike Milligan

M & J. Hobbs ~ Publishers
Surrey

5 September 1982

Dear Spike,

Your letter of the 1st September came like a bolt from the blue.

I have been publishing most of your books since 'The Saga of the Six Gun' by your father in 1968.

In 1971 when the sales of your books warranted larger production and distribution facilities, and I was spending a year producing 'Milligan's Ark', I advised you to approach Michael Joseph with the War Biography.

At the same time I formed a co-publishing business contract with Michael Joseph to distribute my existing titles and any future books – A contract which does not affect your earnings – I take no part of your royalty, nor do you pay me in any way.

I have had this co-publishing arrangement, not uncommon in the trade, not only with your books but also with Harry Secombe, Eric Sykes, Ronnie Corbett, Johnny Speight, Spike Mullins, Marty Feldman and many others.

You say you want my business arrangement with Michael Joseph to cease as of your letter.

I can only think that what you really mean is that you want me to cease being your publisher.

This puzzles me as at your request I am involved in researching and planning two books for you at the moment.

With regard to Carol Barker, the royalty split was agreed between Spike Milligan Productions and Carol Barker's agent – otherwise it would not be in the contract – I certainly don't get any part of it. We can adjust the percentage if necessary.

Best wishes as ever,
Jack

[Remember Jack was a lifelong friend and in my opinion it was a betrayal, and I told Spike so.]

[Now he brings me into the picture because he has started to defend himself, and as he used to say 'I'll need you for back up'.]

Jack Hobbs Esq.
Surrey

13 October 1982

Dear Jack,

I hear from Norma that you are avoiding me. Why? I'm not a leper. I am a human being, I am still a friend of yours.

We agreed on the phone we would go ahead with THERE'S A LOT OF IT ABOUT, because this was going before I wrote the letter to you and Michael Joseph asking to draw up a new arrangement. Since then I have spoken to you on the phone, and when I said we would go ahead with this, you didn't say 'No', in fact, you agreed to do it. Now, I hear you have sent all the stuff to Michael Joseph, and I am totally baffled.

I mean, all I said I wanted to form my own book company, I have a right to do what I want in my life, don't you? I mean, because you introduced me to Michael Joseph, it doesn't mean you have domain over me, I could have gone to another publisher who would have published my books. I explained to you over the phone that I wanted to retire next year, and therefore, my income would drop about 60% and I wanted to earn as much money from my books as I could. I am sorry I can't move into a workhouse for you and live a lesser life, but I do hope you understand I have to survive.

I am just a bit stunned that anybody could be so small minded, you have done very well out of my books, and I am grateful, why can't we go on doing the odd book.

Love, light and peace,
Spike Milligan

M. & J. Hobbs ~ Publishers
Surrey

18 October 1982

Dear Spike,

Thank you for your letter of 13th October. I have been waiting for a reply to my letter of the 5th September for some time. As I told you on the phone I was confused by your attitude. I did not agree to do anything with regard to 'There's a Lot of it About' when you phoned me except order some photographs, and I had sent all the material for all your books back to Michael Joseph's weeks ago after your letter of the 1st September.

I believe Dick was trying to have a meeting with you to sort out what the 'renegotiation' mentioned in your letter would mean to us all. No terms of renegotiation have reached me from any source whatsoever.

I was dismissed as your publisher in no uncertain terms as of the date of your letter of 1st September, and have had to take that at its face value.

Certainly you have the right to form your own publishing company. I don't claim domain over you. I have enjoyed being your publisher over the last fourteen years and am sorry that it has to come to an end.

I have been an independent publisher for thirty years and intend to continue producing books. I don't see any point in doing 'the odd book' when you have your own company so I think we had best make a clean break of it. I'm sorry you think me small minded – I don't quite understand why; and to suggest that if I continued to publish you, you might move into a workhouse is a ludicrously comic piece of overstatement. I have no doubts whatsoever about your ability to survive.

I feel we did some good books together which, but for us, would not be in the British Museum.

Good luck in your new venture, as ever,
Jack

P. S. Re Mangles – I would be grateful if you would return my
   reference books to Orme Court and I will arrange to have
   them collected – many thanks.

*[What a nice man. No wonder I was fond of him. But the hurt between the
lines.]*

———————◆———————

Jack Hobbs Esq.
Surrey

                                           22 October 1982

Dear Jack,

If ever anybody tried desperately to get in touch with another
person, it's me trying to get in touch with you. Finally I spoke on
the phone from Ireland to Norma, who has spoken to you, and
you asked her what I meant by the odd book. When I say we
could do the odd book together you know we wrote McGonagall
books, well I would consider us doing one of these again, and
you can be the joint publisher on it.

   This move by me is actually to try and increase my livelihood,
writing might possibly be my only form of income when I am 65,
and I could not survive unless I did it, and turn out more books.
I do hope you understand.

   When I said I would end up in a workhouse, I wasn't joking,
even now, working full time in television, radio and doing stage
shows, I was overdrawn at the bank last week by £4,000, and if
I had been relying only on my book royalties, I would have been
bankrupt Jack.

This is not a hard luck story, this is the truth, and Norma will verify this.

Anyhow I desperately want to see you again and have dinner and have a laugh. I will not feel happy until I see you again as a friend.

Sincerely,
Spike Milligan
Dictated over the phone and signed in his absence

[Milligan in his contrite mood was always so.]

———•———

Dick Douglas-Boyd Esq.
Michael Joseph & Co.
London WC1

30 October 1981

Dear Doug Dickless,

So you are wearing two hats, I trust this involves an extra pay cheque.

Joke: Doctor to Irishman: Have you had a medical check.
Irishman: Yes, it was for £3. 10 for a truss. End of joke.

Yes, look forward to the free hot dinner, bearing in mind this time I am a vegetarian, don't like dry white wines, and boring bloody salesmen like the last one I sat next to.

I am looking forward to the Wales/Australia match at Cardiff.

I am in an appalling dull mood, and I don't wish to write further.

Love,
Spine Millagnal

———•———

Michael Joseph Ltd
London WC1
Registered Office

15 October 1981

Dear Spike,

I think SCUNTHORPE looks splendid and I hope very much that we will be meeting around publication time at signing sessions. I would certainly like to have a celebratory dinner on or near publication day if you are free (Nov. 2nd).

You probably know that Alan Samson is leaving us to further his career elsewhere and we are sorry to see him go. We have put the day to day handling of your work in the Editorial Department in the hands of Jennie Davies, who has a rather wicked sense of humour, a nice smile and of course the right professional qualifications. Perhaps we could arrange for her to come along to the publication day celebration at which I would also like to introduce you to Karen Geary, who masterminds our Publicity at this end.

You probably saw from the trade press that I had been appointed Publisher for Pelham Books, which as you know is primarily a sporting and leisure imprint. Not a bad position to reach for someone whose major sporting achievement was to be happy hooker for Clifton's Extra Bs. I am looking forward to it immensely. I am of course retaining my MJ responsibilities at least for the time being, and you and Norma know that I am always here in this building should either of you want me.

I have a lovely Irish joke for you, which can probably wait till we meet.

Warmest regards.

Yours,
R. Douglas-Boyd

[Jeremy Robson had asked Spike to confirm that Bill Tidy had his blessing as illustrator of The Melting Pot.*]*

Jeremy Robson Esq.
Robson Books Limited
London W1

22 November 1982

Dear Jeremy,

Let me allay your Jewish business fears. Bill Tidy is possibly one of the finest cartoonists in England, and I have no doubt that his work does not need an audition. Of course, you can if you want to have it auditioned, we could book Drury Lane, and we could have him up on the stage, and say 'do something funny'.

Don't worry, I should go ahead with this, I think it will be a successful book, but check with Norma about the publication date, so it does not clash with my other books. I hope all goes well with you.

Let me recount an incredible incident which occurred up here in Birmingham, Dame Edna Everidge was signing books at Hudsons, and for some reason she had three Policemen in attendance for a crowd who numbered about 35. For a joke I dressed up as a drunken Australian, with a hat with corks all around, and I went there claiming to be her husband Norm, and bugger me, they threw me out, would you believe it. But, next day I had my revenge, when I was signing my own books at Boots, and had a crowd of 892, and it took me four hours to do the signing. I think it might all go well for our future project.

Lots of love to you and your family, and of course, your Mum and Dad, and, of course, your Bank Manager.

As ever
Spike Milligan

[I refused to be a director of Monkenhurst books. He wanted me to run it, and be managing director. I refused, told him I had too much respect for Jack and Dick and it was a betrayal. He wanted me to approach Dick and I refused. This was the letter to return.]

Dick Douglas-Boyd Esq.
Pelham Books Limited
London WC1

20 December 1982

Dear Doug Dickless,

I had a meeting with the 'directors' of Monkenhurst Books, and they showed me all the terrifying pitfalls of going into partnership with you to publish my next book. I do not have the time to investigate the agenda in minute detail; on the strength of it I am handing it over, the whole of 'There's a lot of it about' to Michael Joseph to market as per author and publisher.

I originally asked Jack Hobbs to do this, but when I announced that on future books I would try and publish through my own Company, he threw a 'huff', and decided not to have anymore to do with me. So fairs the human race in friendship.

I am passing it over to you, Jennie Davies has all the manuscripts/literature/photographs etc., so if that is OK with you, I would like you to forward the contract to Norma, and we will proceed on that basis.

As ever,
Spike Milligan

Jack Hobbs Esq.
Surrey

17 January 1983

Dear Jack,

I have tried to trace your grave without much success. However, here's something which might bring you back from the dead.

You know I wanted to start my own Book Company because retiring at 65, I might need the bread. I formed a Company and was then told by all the people in it that it would be a total failure, and the effort would not be worth the money, so I have closed it down again – jolly good.

Next, I hear that Dick Douglas-Boyd is delighted I have closed it down again, and asked me the vital question 'May I approach Jack and ask him to re-establish the joint publisher relationship'.

Well, I thought, rather than him do it, I will do it. Do you think you could recover from your sudden death, and cataclysmic tragedy, with its world shaking implications upon you and your underwear, and your fucking bank manager. I will be delighted to re-unite us whereby which you can start transporting hundredweights of vital books into my house, so I can look for Victorian Mangles, and then I can have them transported back, where they will lie mouldering in Norma's office. You can tell the difference, Norma is the one that smokes.

Sincerely,
Spike Milligan

[The act of contrition. – Mind you, well put.]

Ms Jennie Davies
Michael Joseph Limited
London WC1

5 June 1985

Dear Jennie,

I have seen the shock horror picture on the front of the
Bookseller, the only alternative to this could be Quasi Modo
himself. I mean, why don't we see Kingsley Amis dressed up as
an Admiral with wooden legs, to sell his books.

    Anyhow I am going along with it only because you are very
very beautiful, but if you were ugly I would have a picture of
Robert Redford superimposed over my face, as being The Real
Spike Milligan.

    Tell me has Michael Joseph sunk so low that they have me on
the front of the Bookseller – what has gone wrong. Please tell me
has the Diary of an Edwardian Lady come to an end.

Love, light and peace,
Spike Milligan

WHERE HAVE ALL THE BULLETS GONE?

SPIKE MILLIGAN

The fifth volume of his hilarious, bestselling autobiography

Write - for M.Joseph
5 Summers

MICHAEL JOSEPH LTD

44 Bedford Square London WC1B 3DP. Telephone: 01-323 3200 Telex: 21322 Telegrams: Emjaybuks London WC1
Registered Office   Registered in England No. 304766

250 words   September

(N) See over

Spike Milligan Esq
Spike Milligan Productions Ltd
9 Orme Court
London W2

July 23rd, 1985

Dear Spike,

As you know, it's our fiftieth anniversary next year and I have been asked by
the board to write and ask you if you would be prepared to contribute to a small
celebratory book that we shall be publishing in March.

The aim is an affectionate, amusing and light-hearted look at the beginnings
and career of the firm over the past fifty years and we shall be including
some selections from already published memoirs, a piece by Michael Joseph
himself, one by Richard Joseph on his father and, we hope, a number of amusing
stories from celebrated authors and associates.

I do hope that you may have a short story to tell, either about the firm or
about Michael Joseph. We'd ideally like about 250 words by September at the
latest.

Let me know what you can produce. It would be lovely to have a contribution
from you - in fact, the book would be incomplete without one.

Love,

Jennie

Jennie Davies

Spike loved J. B. Morton, so he was delighted to play Beachcomber. BBC2, 1969.

Spike always told me Pete was good-looking. *Ghost in the Noonday Sun*, Kyrenia, 1973.

1977, *Guardian* newspaper commercial. Still dressed from Oxfam.

When I showed Spike this photo he actually said: 'Tony Benn is a great human being; a bit eccentric, though.' Couldn't believe my ears.

Alan Clare, one of *my* favourite people. He was a true friend to Spike.

His one-man show, 1974.
Adelphi Theatre, London.

Japanese embassy, 1976.
Demonstration for 'Save
the Whales'. Oxfam really
doing well.

Who he? Filming with
Marty Feldman. Marty
didn't recognize Spike.

1977 Going-away dinner for Spike's mother's return to Australia.
Sile, Mrs Reid (the children's nanny), Sean, Laura, Grandma
Milligan, Spike, Paddy and Jane.

Spike with his hero, Woody Herman – no, not Michael Parkinson.
Mind you, he thought 'Parky' was 'a good lad'.

Keeping himself fit for the 'Bayswater harem' (my name for his girlfriends).

'I write them. Now I have to sell them and sign them.' Say cheese and get on with it. At a signing session in 1978.

Spike auditioning for the part of Monty's double. Didn't get it, so he wrote *Monty: His Part in My Victory*.

Prince Charles and Diana's wedding, 1981. The policeman has been told to keep an eye on him.

This Is Your Life – second time with 'My Old Mate' Eric.
Spike still being dressed by Oxfam (*c.*1995).

Sir George Martin.
Not only was he Spike's
best man at his second
marriage but George
could do no wrong.
So when Spike was
asked to present an award
to him he was thrilled.
He was always so proud
of George.

Johnny Speight's funeral, 1998. We look quite friendly holding hands
– what went wrong? Well, it would only be for five minutes.

At an *Oldie* Lunch (*c.*1998): Milligan and O'Toole. Two old fakes.
They insist they are Irish. Milligan born in India; O'Toole born in Leeds.
Nonetheless, two loveable rogues.

250 words! No - but I'll write as much as I can
What am I, a millionaire prankster doing writing
books for Michael Josephs, it came about by strange
decree, I had written a MS, ~~the~~ on W W II, I thumbed it
round publishers, who treated me like Hitler at a
a ~~Bamitzfa~~ Barmitzva. Finnaly I trundled round hander
on a barrow, selling it page at a time, then I remembered
I had forgotten Collins, this company manager wanted
to meet me on a Saturday at his flat, fearfull of Aids
Herpes and La Grippe, I declined, & I knew there was this
firm called Michael Josephs who only published books
by Edwardian Lady Naturalists who threw themselves into
their work and rivers, so disguising myself as Doris
Milligan, lady artist and laundry woman - I managed
to get an interview with an ageing editor Doug
Dickless Boyd, then in his 90th year, who went round fallen women, carrying homes
a matress, with a card. ladies serviced while you wait.
I entered his office that reeked of Steredent and
Condoms, I waited till he'd finished, and she had
left, 'Now' he said'. I need 20 minutes rest and some
old mens hormones. I will say this of him, for a man
who was nude he showed remarkable calm: In
short I told him I wasn't a woman and the
swelling went down - in that weak moment
I sang him 'Hitler my part in his down fall' - forcing
my hand onto a powerful contract. which gave
me I percent after the 1st ten million - he counter signed
and saying 'You one of ours now' chained me to
a filing cabinet where I have remained this
20 years

S Milligan

['Millionaire Prankster' was Private Eye's name for Spike.]

Ms Anne Ainley
Puffin Books Limited
London W8

19 January 1987

Dear Anne,

My Manager has forwarded me a letter which you sent to me, which did get to her, and finally from her to me; no wonder there is three million unemployed.

By all means do what you think necessary to make the book more saleable; personally I resent having to excise it from the book because it was written in all innocence, and there are such things as black people, and there are such things as black people with no clothes on, and there are such things as black people with bones through their nose, so everything is basically a fact. However, in the light of commercial enterprise, I give way.

I don't have time to do a new illustration, so just take the lot out of the book – and we give way to the looney left.

Sincerely, looney right,
Spike Milligan

[See the letter of 3 June 1982 above.]

Ms Susan Watt
Michael Joseph
London W8

23 February 1993

Dear Susan,

Louise came to see me to talk over the bible, all was well except the editing out all the references to God. Now in no case did I blaspheme God, all my references are comic and innocent – there was only one in which I called God a two faced shit, this I agree should be edited out but the others, as I say, are comic.

You must realise no matter *how* you edit this book lots of people will find it offensive, but this will be wonderful publicity for the book; so please edit, not in fear, but with intelligence.

Love, light and peace,
Spike Milligan

P. S. Likewise can we keep in David Napley's name and not use Rumpole of the Bailey.

[The Bible according to Spike Milligan. The Publishers wanted to edit the word God. Which was ludicrous.]

I write this foreward in fear and trepidation,
the fear is that having turned the old testament
into a comedy, I will become the Roman Catholic
Salmon Rushdie, and, on publication of
the work I will receive a fatwah from the
Pope. Why did I write it as a comedy?
the simple answer is it was about time.
I refer to the old testament, the hours
mounting to days, as a child I was
forced to read (many times aloud) chapter
after chapter of blood, thunder, fornication
scheming greed murder, rape arson, and sometimes dirty dancing I admit as a
child I was deeply impressed by it all, it was
like Hollywood movie, I remember I was
in awe of Samson   who slew thousands
with the asses jaw bone, I imagined every
single conflict as he smote (smote bible in word)
I thrilled to David killings Goliath (hundred
of cubits high) with a sling shot (in
down town Gaza they're still in use). time
passed, and the a memory of the old testament
faded, like well was underpants, faded

However throughout the Christian world
the good book is still read by millions, ~~so~~
~~now~~ the book itself is in the main pretty
gloomy, tedious, unendingly nefarious, nearly
all those in it have blood on their hands, so
recently I would jolly it up, I know lots
^though
of people will be offended, sorry about that,
but lots of people will laugh, and thats
~~ot. ~~~~~~~~~~~~ about that. Amen

12

The Jimmy Verner Affair

JIMMY VERNER = ONE MAN STAGE

~~JAMES~~ 21ST AUGUST. MAYFAIR

21 — 1ST CHARITY. ~~MENTALL~~ HANDICAPPED) CHILD.
                                    PILGRIMAGE TRUST

22 . 2ND) . ~~MENTALLY~~ HANDICAPPED)
                                    ADULTS.

7½ WEEKS. TO 11TH OCTOBER.

THEN NORWICH = THEATRE ROYAL.
       13 OCT — 18TH OCTOBER.

SKIP RICHMOND

_____

[Me trying to get those dates in his diary. Failing miserably. The start of his one man show.]

3-7-80.

JIMMY VERNER:

1 WEEK RICHMOND} 1ST SEPT.
          THEATRE   FINISH 6 SEPT.

5 WEEKS MAYFAIR   8TH SEPT.
          THEATRE   FINISH 11 OCTOBER.

1 WEEK NORWICH } 13 OCTOBER
          THEATRE ROYAL   FINISH 18 OCT.

TALK TO ME ABOUT MAYFAIR
310 SEATS ONLY.
JIMMY HAS THEATRES - NOW

BILLING SECOND HALF.
     VERY CLEAR = DON'T APPEAR UNTIL
               SECOND.

31- 7- 80.

HAROLD WILSON MASK:
THEY DO NOT HAVE ONE
IN STOCK. WOULD YOU
LIKE THEM TO MAKE ONE
SPECIALLY. TAKE COUPLE OF
WEEKS TO GET MOULD RIGHT.

YES -   NO

[Start of his props for the show.]

James Verner

c/o May Fair Theatre
Stratton Street
London W1

(...BUT ONLY JUST!!)

3rd September 1980

Spike Milligan Esq
9 Orme Court
London W2

Dear Spike,

I enclose a copy of a letter to me from Ashley Parker,
together with a copy of my reply. Let me add to this
the enquiries from Alan Clare and Jamie Jauncey - not
to mention the interest my assistant (hired for the
occasion) and Production Stage Manager, Tony Walters,
have in the Show.

I said I was happy to wait until you were ready, and
indeed that was so, but this was based on a knowledge of
your professional commitments at that time and your own
expressed interest in doing the show.   I now understand
that a film has cropped up for September and October
- not in my calculations at all - and I have to ask you
the following:

Would you please give me a date to open the Show between
November 16th and November 25th this year, and can I have
this date agreed by next Monday, 8th September.

I must advise the people in the first paragraph of my letter
exactly what the situation is, because as you will appreciate
their livelihood and future employment depends on this information.

I was delighted to hear the Mel Brooks film went so well.

How about dinner next week?

Yours,

James Verner

encs:

[handwritten notes:]

HAVE SAID NORMA WILL FIX

DATE ON MONDAY.

(N) We can't go on like
this — he wants a
DATE — he can't give it
so CANCEL — But →

I will still try and get the one man
show together — under the
impossible circumstances I live in
— But I'll do it with him.

[Jimmy waited eighteen months and we started all over again.]

30 - 10 - 80.

SPIKE— CAN I TALK TO
YOU. RE ATTACHED) LETTER
FROM JIMMY VERNER.
I THINK, ON A BUSINESS
LEVEL, WE SHOULD) PAY SOMETHING.
ATTACHED) ALSO BREAKDOWN. I CAN
NEGOTIATE STAFF FIGURES.

Go Ahead.
You deal.

———◆———

James Verner Esq.
London W1

25 August 1982

Dear Jimmy,

I was absolutely destroyed when I read your letter. Briefly if I can recall the story, you tried to help me put on a One Man Show, alas while we were trying to do it I seemed not to be able to get enough time to rehearse it, and a badly rehearsed show would have been disastrous for all of us.

Now I am an actor not a manager, and my manager is supposed to manage me and my affairs to my advantage and not to bring about any bad feeling. This obviously has not happened.

Regarding the finances, and 'recoup our losses', I was given to understand by Norma Farnes that she had negotiated your part of the loss and that she had made it good, so that will have to be a question you will have to ask her.

Regarding flying back from LA, well I knew nothing about this, basically all I understood was we were going to put on a show, and it didn't come off, and if ever we did it again I would put it on in London. Norma must have known about this, and she should have raised the question what about Jimmy Verner. Alas, nobody has approached me since about doing a One Man Show, and Has I had already done a show with Pat O'Neill in Australia, and I was doing, nothing, but nothing regarding earning a living, I was glad when he came up with this.

Needless to say I accepted it, but as I say my Manager should have said to me 'What about Jimmy Verner'.

I suppose morally I am to blame on the basis of principles, but I assure you I have not done it with any malicious intent, I did it because it was an offer of work, and the conditions were right for me to do it.

Would you please write and let me know do I owe you any money because if you haven't been paid then I will make sure you do.

I am sorry, it's the thing called 'showbusiness'. The last thing I would want to do was to hurt you, and perhaps I have, and I feel pretty bloody.

Alas, the die is cast, and I can't go back on it.

As ever,
Spike Milligan

[Norma in the dock. I call it passing the buck. He excelled at that.]

25 August 1982

Dear Spike,

Please, please understand why I have to write this letter,
I couldn't talk to you on the telephone today because you
were too upset.

I will take full responsibility for the Jimmy Verner affair, that's
my job, and the letter has already gone off to him, your copy
attached.

I think, deep inside, you know I am 100% loyal to you, and to
myself I have 100% professional integrity, so for my own peace of
mind I have to send this letter to say, when you told me that Pat
O'Neill was going to do the tour of your One Man Show, I said to
you 'Spike, what about Jimmy Verner, we promised him', and you
said 'Fuck him', and went on to talk about Pat O'Neill. I realised it
was too late, and that there was nothing I could do.

I am certainly not bringing anyone else into this, it's not my
style, but Tanis knows, and knows how worried I've been about
Jimmy Verner finding out – hence my note on his letter to you
saying – 'I've been waiting for this'.

There's absolutely no need to mention this ever again, destroy
the letter and forget it, but try to understand it was only for my
peace of mind.

Love,
Norma

[He was ill, one of the black dog Periods when normally I would not disturb him. But another act of betrayal and he knew it. But ill or not I felt very deeply about this and he had to know. Jimmy Verner was one of my favourite people and Spike knew that.]

James Verner Esq.
London W1

20 December 1982

Dear Jimmy,

I have a guilty conscience about not putting on the original show
I intended with you (for no other reason than there was no
bloody time).

I am given to understand from Norma that you are £1,500 out
of pocket, and I am writing to tell you that I intend paying this
just as soon as I have that capital available.

I do hope that you are still not too annoyed, because I am not
a bad person, I get pretty mixed up with modern day living, and
I still think you are a great bloke, but you are allowed to call me a
shit another eight times, but after that it has to stop.

As ever,
Spike Milligan

[Another act of contrition. He was a professor of that.]

James Verner
Has To Be
Better Than 2
And Bigger!

4th January 1983

Dear Spike,

Firstly, not even once 'a shit', although until I got your letter I was
wondering where I stood with you – or do I mean sat.

I am delighted that you are sending me the balance outstanding on our last attempt to work together not least because they are cutting off my phone on Friday so that I can't even talk about putting a show on let alone going through the hell of trying. (have been working on a musical called 'Utopia' for months – would *you* like to play King Paramount of Utopia for a few months ???)

Hope to do something with you this year, whatever . . .

Yours,
James Verner

———◆———

James Verner Esq.
Curzon Productions International Inc.
London W1

24 January 1983

My dear Jimmy, or might I say, Dearest Jimmy,

Over the incident, as you know I feel so terrible about it, I want you to know that I think you are a great guy, what happened to you, via me, made me feel a bit of a shit. I just wanted to tell you how sorry I was. I'll put you out of your misery now, I can't do Utopia, for the simple reason I am writing a novel, and the publishers have given me an advance on it, otherwise, I think I would most certainly be interested in doing it, but might I point out, and this may make you lose some of your morale, putting on Gilbert & Sullivan at the same time as Pirates of Penzance is running at Drury Lane, I think is a bad move, it would have been much better to wait, let the momentum come and go, then they have got the taste for up-dated G. and S., before putting yours on.

Of course, you know damn well I wish it every success in the world, and if you tell me where the rehearsals are taking place, I will try and pop down and suggest some ideas, that is with the acceptance of all the tempremental Queens and Producers etc, if I can be of any help, and thank you very much for the offer.

I am sending you another £500 to pay off what I owe you, and I think eventually I should pay the interest what would have been on this money.

Why didn't you come and see me after the show, I would have liked that, and I would have felt much better if I could shake your hand. Whilst dictating this letter Norma tells me that you did come back to see me, but 'a man' (who are these fucking men that fuck up the world), said I was waiting for an urgent call, that was all shit, it's amazing that even my girlfriend Shelagh, and Pat O'Neill, and all the nanas in show business just don't know when to recognise a real show business person, and put around such a thin fucking story.

Anyhow, I am sorry that happened, if I go on any further saying I'm sorry, I will be saying I'm sorry for burning the Jews at Auschwitz.

The appalling part of showbusiness I notice, it's the in-between people who fuck it up totally.

I am certain that if Jesus Christ himself got on the telephone and Tanis answered she would put him off.

Love, light and peace,
Spike Milligan

P. S. In the next couple of weeks I would love to take you to din- ner, and come and see a rehearsal. Some ideas which I think might be funny is one or two of the main characters, that is the most unlikely ones, might carry sex dummies under his arm, whilst singing an Aria, but carries it throughout the show. Others could carry appalling C & A Modes shopping bags, and one could clutch a violin throughout the whole show, and never play it. I also thought that during the whole show you might have a large television on the side of the stage, during which some of the cast not involved would be watching Coronation Street or Dallas.

[Well, Well. Acts of contrition don't get better than this.]

13

Broadcasting – His Opinions

Messrs Frank Muir & Dennis Norden
BBC Television Centre
London W12

20 April 1959

Dear Frank and Dennis,

I had fancied myself at one time as a comedy writer, but at the time of writing no-one else in the world does, except a firm in Australia where I am going this summer!

I should like to do some television shows for the BBC. I have got absolutely nowhere with the top brass who have got the illusion that I am difficult – a word that is always dispensed when people don't understand what you are trying to do. I had intended to write to Eric Maschwitz, but I don't speak Russian (the joke is a reference to the Balaleika of course).

What does one have to do to get a T. V. half hour in which one is allowed to produce the comedy and the camera angles so that the public might get the best effect?

This is in effect my swan song as far as trying to get a show on BBC TV. On what happens as a result of this letter depends whether I ever work for them again.

I am writing to you because you are writers and might understand how important it is to myself not to let some producer cock up my endeavours, which you know is so easily done. Anyhow, write and let me know. I sail on the 24th of this month.

Sincerely,
Spike Milligan

———•———

Frank Muir & Denis Norden
London W1

22 April 1959

Dear Spike,

This is just to underline our telephone conversation, following your letter.

By the time you get back from Australia we should be securely enough entrenched in this BBC appointment to be able to back up any assurances we make. All we can say now is that we would welcome the opportunity of helping you get some of your weird and wonderful ideas on BBC TV.

Meantime, have a good skive in the Antipodes and come back refreshed in mind and pocket.

Yours,
Frank Muir and Denis Norden

———•———

Denis Mitchell Esq.
BBC Television Centre
London W12

23 April 1959

Dear Denis Mitchell,

I always keep my television in the toilet because most of the subject matter is best fitted to that little precinct.

I must tell you that your 'Soho Story' was magnificent, one of the most marvellous pieces of television to date. I think that's about all.

Sincerely,
Spike Milligan

P. S. How did you manage to get it past your idiot hierarchy?

———◆———

The British Broadcasting Corporation
Television Studios: Lime Grove
London, W12

29 April 1959

Dear Spike Milligan,

For 17 years I've been trying to convince my daughter that I'm an Okay figure. Your letter may have done the trick at last, you being part of a revered Trinity; (the others are Dave Brubeck and whoever wrote 'The Dud Avocado'.) Thank you very much.

I'm going to Africa this week for three months. May I ring you when I get back? There's many a thing I'd like to talk to you about, if you could spare the time.

Sincerely,
Denis Mitchell

Charles Chilton, Esq.
BBC
Aeolian Hall
London W1

1 May 1963

Dear Charles,

Thank you for coming along to lunch, I would like to reiterate exactly how I feel about the prospect of a short sound series.

I would like to write six half-hours using as a basis some of the best of the original shows I have written in Australia, on my three separate visits there. The basis of the show would be to use the Australian idiom, which would mean using a semi Australian cast. I do not think this has been done before on BBC Light Entertainment, and I think the idea should be a success, as the shows in question will be the best of some 42 shows, all of which were a success in Australia.

It is no good the BBC comparing these shows to the old 'Goon Shows', as they did do when I originally submitted them some two years ago. I will guarantee them personally, as being a success. I would like to assure the powers that be, that I have every confidence in my own ability, even if perhaps they do not. However, the six shows that I have in mind, would be: (1) The Flying Dustman Series, (2) The Story behind the last Test, (3) The

Son of Ned Kelly, (4) The Story of Australia's Challenge for the America Cup, (5) The Twergled Englishman, (6) The Missing Australian Prime Minister's Trousers.

Of course the BBC would have to be made aware that these shows could not be transcriptioned nor repeated in Australia, as they have already heard them, but that would be the only difference as far as the contract went.

I hope that they will consider these programmes, for my money I should like to do them this coming autumn, starting November and running into the Christmas week. I know that the BBC are conditioned to think in terms of 13 programmes, but I do not see why this should stop them getting 6 very funny shows, and a personal guarantee of their success.

I think that's all.

As ever,
Spike Milligan

———•———

Holmes Tolley, Esq.
Warwickshire

9 November 1966

Dear Mr Tolley,

I am puzzled as to why the BBC, the people I presume would pay me, have not contacted me themselves, are they using you as a portable plastic runabout.

Yes, in principle I will do it, but

1) who is going to interview me? Normally some twit with elastic legs comes in with a portable tape recorder; first he does not know how it works except for switching it on and off, therefore, after having 15 years of this 'I'm sorry it was not recording that time etc.' there will be only one take.

Can we have an interviewer, not to come armed with these
dreary cliches, 'Tell me Mr Milligan what did you think of etc.
etc.' I would like somebody to consider me: an intelligent human
being, and not a chatty, chubby idiot.

As to the price, my normal fee *was* 15 gns, these days I get 30 gns.

In the light of what I have said, are you and/or the BBC still
interested.

Sincerely,
Spike Milligan

———•———

Duncan Wood Esq.
British Broadcasting Corporation
London W12

6 December 1967

Dear Duncan,

I have received the script on the 6th December. Would you
clarify with Michael Mills what part I am playing because he
thinks I should be playing Cocklecarrots and you don't, and I
should like to know which one of you is going to win. Just so
I can learn the words properly. The sooner the better because
I take a long time to learn lines.

Also the Beachcomber speech which is done straight at
camera, I presume, can we have a tele-prompt with that so I can
spend more time learning lines of any characters I play.

Sincerely,
Spike Milligan
Dictated by Spike Milligan and signed in his absence

———•———

E. K. Wilson Esq.
British Broadcasting Corporation
Kensington House
London W14

6 December 1967

Dear Pat Wilson,

You may have noticed that I have never gone in for what I call long term television, to become involved in what becomes a series. It's death to a long professional life. This is why I avoid, in any shape or form, entering into half hour series on a long term basis.

Apart from which, I diversify my talents between writing books, plays and appearing on the stage.

I think if I were to allow you to take up an option it would negate these two latter practices, and upset my very cautious planning act in what is a very tenuous profession.

So I'm afraid I will have to say 'no'; I took a long time to say it which means I feel for you.

However, once the thing is a success that success can not be obliterated and if next year or in the foreseeable future you would like to repeat it, at a time mutually advantageous. I would be only too willing to take up the torch.

Sincerely,
Spike Milligan
Dictated by Spike Milligan and signed in his absence

J. Burton, Esq.
The Natural History Unit
British Broadcasting Corporation
Bristol

17 May 1972

Dear John,

There is a blackbird at the back of my office who is a magnificent singer, in the mornings (Dawn Chorus) and evenings.

I am not particularly conversant with how good blackbirds are, but this one seems to me to be a wonderful singer.

I thought perhaps if you were up here you might like to record him for posterity. I call him Frank Sinatra.

Do let me know.

Love, Light, and Peace,   *S) John is coming to record. (N)*
Spike Milligan

———◆———

Billy Cotton Jnr Esq.
British Broadcasting Corporation
Television Centre
London W12

15 March 1973

Dear Bill,

What are you doing to poor Cilla Black? She is a very good singer and they ought to give her an all musical show but I mean NAAFI night out – I mean I can play Abide with Me on the bones. I am not trying to be rude but I am a great Cilla fan and think that she is one of the great singing talents.

We all drew lots in the office as to who would write this letter, I won.

Love, Light and Peace,
Spike Milligan

P. S. You did not black up for your appearance, everyone recognized you right away. Invite me to the club for one of those 'darling you were wonderful' meetings.

[He thought Cilla was great and deserved better, and thought Billy should know.]

Frank Gillard Esq.
Somerset

6 June 1974

Dear Mr Gillard,

In answer to your letter of the 1st April, 1969; in this letter you were defending the BBC's reason as to find me unsuitable to appear on Family Choice. Since that letter I have been on Family Choice, and I want to know what happened that suddenly made me acceptable. You see I am like a bulldog and I never let go, and whereas I don't suppose you can give me an answer, I am just pointing out that sometimes what the BBC says and believes one day, it doesn't believe the next, and this makes the truth very very difficult to find.

Briefly what the BBC was saying, was 'this man is not fit to put on records and read postcards'. I am certain everybody in my

profession in the last 20 years has done a record programme and
I believe that it was a personal dislike that led them to exclude
me from this programme for so long.

Just to fill you in, when they finally agreed to let me do
Open House,* even though it was a live programme they insisted
that I was pre-recorded and then I only appeared for half the
programme. When the Times Radio critic asked why, a BBC
Spokesman said 'that this was so', the brilliant two faced answer
was 'it was a gimmick'.

The reason why I pursued this course from the year 1960 to
1969 was to prove conclusively that there is a point in the
bureaucracy where there is no logic, just personal dislike, and
nobody will come out with the truth at the beginning and say
'I don't like this man', if they do this it would be very easy to
accept it, but to stall for nine years I find asinine.

I hope you are enjoying your retirement, I don't intend to.

Sincerely,
Spike Milligan

[Tenacious bulldog or what?]

Frank Gillard

7 June 1974

Dear Spike,

I can only tell you that you have been one of my favourite people
ever since the day you came to lunch with Hugh Greene at
Broadcasting House and brought some bottles of excellent wine
along with you. So be assured that there was never the slightest

* The follow on from *Family Choice*.

question of personal prejudice on my part, and I never heard
anything of the kind expressed by any of my colleagues.
Had any of them taken that line, I should have been rather
rough with them. I am delighted to know that you broke
through the barrier, whatever it was made of, and that you have
entertained the nation on Family Choice. I wish I had heard it.
Probably I was abroad. I work a good deal in America these days,
and in fact I am off over there again now, within a matter of
hours.

How right you are about retirement. I have certainly not
retired. I left the BBC at the age deadline, but started at once
on other work which I find utterly absorbing and satisfying.
You will not even have to make that sort of change. Just keep
going on. That's what we Milligan fanatics ask of you.

Yours,
Frank

———•———

Frank Gillard Esq.
Somerset

12 June 1974

Dear Frank,

Thank you for your letter. I have never suggested that you had
the slightest prejudice against me, but *there's no doubt about it
somebody did*, and that amounts to emotional fascism.

Alas, I have never found out who the person was who held me in such horror, but believe me it leaves a mark on a person when you are not considered trustworthy enough to play a few gramophone records, and I find that unbelievable.

Hope you enjoy your new job, I still have my old one.

Love, light and peace,
Spike Milligan

[Obsessive or just won't let go.]

BRITISH BROADCASTING CORPORATION
BROADCASTING HOUSE LONDON W1A 1AA
TELEPHONE 01-580 4468 TELEX: 22182
TELEGRAMS AND CABLES: BROADCASTS LONDON TELEX
12th May 1975

Dear Miss Farnes,

Following our telephone conversation today I enclose
the script of <u>Badjelly the Witch</u>. The policy principle I
have to work to does not allow the mingling of 'fact' and
'fiction', i.e. God and Badjelly (see pages 13-14); so
would Mr Milligan be kind enough to accept my reluctantly
bodged alternative notion of the Sun disposing of Badjelly -
or perhaps provide a better alternative? I would greatly
appreciate an early answer, as production plans are well
advanced. I am sorry to be such a nuisance.

Yours sincerely,

Colin Smith

(Colin Smith)
Producer, <u>Let's Join In</u>.

Miss Norma Farnes,
Spike Milligan Productions Ltd,
9 Orme Court,
London, W. 2.

aa
enc

TALK TO ME

Norma.

*Instead of Sunrise
As it is or NOT
Moonrise!*

*Ann.
'o rancu. 18 feb.*

Colin Smith Esq.
British Broadcasting Corporation
Broadcasting House
London W1

21 May 1975

Dear Colin

LET'S JOIN IN.
BADJELLY THE WITCH.

Norma has explained to me about the changing of the script. I really am sorry, I do not find God unctious, and I just cannot acquiesce to a silly rule. If the BBC are so narrow minded, I am not going to contribute to its stupidity that way.

Sincerely,
Spike Milligan
Dictated by Spike Milligan and signed in his absence

Open File
Goon Show –
with P. Charles ?

BRITISH BROADCASTING CORPORATION
BROADCASTING HOUSE LONDON W1A 1AA
TELEPHONE 01-580 4468   TELEX: 265781
TELEGRAMS AND CABLES: BROADCASTS LONDON TELEX

28th June 1976

Dear Spike,

Welcome back to the colder climes of Europe.

In the last few months there have been developments which will hopefully lead to a very special Goon Show recording in about April of next year.   Before we could ever make positive moves in the several directions necessary we must have your willingness to participate.

John Browell told me of certain assurances that he had had from Peter and Harry in which they had said that April 1977 seems very suitable to them.   Perhaps John will be in touch with you shortly and the whole subject cleared with you, but as far as I am concerned, and at my rarefied level in the BBC, I have to give assurances to the higher masters that everything will fall into shape on the date in question.

Hope to hear from you shortly.

As ever.

Con.

(C.J. Mahoney)
Head of Light Entertainment
Radio

Spike Milligan, Esq.
9 Orme Court
Bayswater
London, W.2

SCP

Tell him – the Goon Show on its own no – but if Charles participated as a performer it would work other wise no are

C. J. Mahoney Esq.
British Broadcasting Corporation
Broadcasting House
London W1

30 June 1976

Dear Con,

Thank you for your letter with your once five yearly employment schedule for me.

I am averse to doing a Goon Show again because it's just digging up the past, and all the energy for this show has been diversified. Therefore, a straight forward Goon Show for me would be a backward step.

However, John Browell has talked to my Manager, Norma Farnes and said the same as you have written except that if I agree to do a Goon Show the BBC would approach Prince Charles to see if he would appear in it. If Prince Charles is approached first and asked if he would appear in it, this, of course, would give an extra dimension, and we would not be so reliant on an old team to bring about passed laughter which we no longer could do.

So the picture is this: if Prince Charles agrees to appear in it I will write a Goon Show, but one on its own would be anti-climaxical, as the last one was, in fact the audience was better than the show.

Hope you understand.

Love, light and peace,
Spike Milligan
Dictated by Spike Milligan and signed in his absence

West Germany

22 June 1977

Dear Spike,

I have now managed to decipher all seven of the Scripts and I must say that, in the main, I find them extremely funny. I am especially pleased to see the re-emergence of Herbert Skrackle as a force to be reckoned with: Herbert and his Co-Directors! My only reservation is that on reading alone I feel that one or two of the longer sketches may be just a little too long. However that is something that will be made clear when we get around to reading and rehearsing them together.

There are one or two Technical points that I should like to mention. Any page numbers I use are the page numbers from your original Scripts.

1. On the question of Music: we will not be able to use Woody Herman's 'Apple Honey' as there is no chance of our being able to clear it even for Commonwealth, let alone World sales. Big Band Music played by a British Band is usually clearable.

2. The Wardrobe and scenery costs are going to be very large, but with a reasonable amount of Doubling-up we should be all right.

3. Remembering our experiences over language in 'The Melting Pot'. I am a bit surprised at so many 'Buggers and Bloodys' turning up. I am afraid they will nearly all have to come out.

4. Because of the number of breaks required for Costume and Make-up changes almost all the 'Quickies' will have to be done on film, either at Ealing or on location. Even so, we shall have to use some valuable Studio rehearsal time on Pre-VTRing several of the Announcer sequences on the day. It's sad about Chris Langham but Keith Smith should make an excellent and very professional replacement in shows 1 to 5.

5. In Show 2 is 'Pissed' on Rewrite page 7 really necessary? I have a sneaking feeling that the diseases Sketch may go on a little too long.

6. In Show 4 who do you want to play Tom Jackson, just in case Mr Jackson himself does not want to play it?

7. In Show 5, halfway down Rewrite page 4 we have the instruction 'We are still in Studio'. However at that point we are

on film and as I see it we do not go back to Studio until half-way
down Rewrite page 5 when Spike is in Studio as an Announcer.
Because of Policy decisions at the BBC people who work in
Sports, Current Affairs or News are not allowed by *their*
Departments to take part in Comedy Shows. This is partly my
own fault in that we made so much use of such people that the
shutters were pulled down a couple of years ago. And so, who
would you like to play Frank Bough in Show 5? And once again
we have 'Bugger', not just once but twice. (I'm sorry, it happens
twice in Show 6, only once in Show 5!)

8. In Show 6, once again, there are too many 'Buggers' and
'Bloodys'. In Show 6, Rewrite Page 13 we will be unlikely to have a
Hand-held Electronic Camera on the set in the Railway station
Sketch. It would cost the Show far too much to have a Hand-held
Unit in the Studio along with our normal Camera Crew.

9. In Show 7, Rewrite page 6, near the top of the page we are on
location in a street with Spike, Dorning and Lodge. The next
instruction is '3 shot in Studio'. Why? Surely this sketch would be
much better continued on film, where a mix to the final Scene of the
sequence with Spike lying in the bed would work perfectly. (This
would also help enormously with Costume and Make-up changes.)

On Rewrite page 12 surely the small scene of Spike on the Concert
Stage, sandwiched between two scenes at Wigmore Hall, should be
on film as well: otherwise we go Film-short Studio-Film and the
quality change becomes very obvious indeed. On Show 7, bottom of
Rewrite Page 16, Henry Cooper, having a very commercially-
minded Agent, will come very expensive for one shot. Could we not
use Nosher Powell, ex-Boxer and Performer instead.

I'm sorry to have had to make so many apparently small
points but they do affect Special Effects, Film Requirements and
Design rather a lot. I'll be seeing you soon and I hope all goes
well with you. All my best to Norma, Neil and Tanis,

Yours Aye,
Ian McNaughton

Ian McNaughton Esq.
British Broadcasting Corporation
Television Centre
London W12

30 June 1977

Dear Hen,

Just to clear up the points you brought up in your letter of the
22nd June, 1977.

I have told John Kilby to alter all the scripts to read Keith
Smith in place of Chris Langham.

OK. Cut out all the 'bloodys', 'buggars', and 'Piss offs',
and the warm up for the show will be done by a Priest. In
place of all the rude words we intend to substitute the names of
furniture, like dutch wardrobe, cracked Regency commode,
Louis XVth Dressing Table, French Escritoire. This we can do
at rehearsals.

Regarding Woody Herman and his band playing Apple Honey,
John Kilby tells me there is no problem using this for the home
broadcast, he also said (which conflicts with your belief), that
'Big Band music played by British Bands is usually clearable'.
Likewise, only usable for home transmission but not overseas or
Commonwealth. So, I am asking the question: – what do we do?
We want music which will allow us to get an overseas repeat.
John Kilby says the only way is to employ a big band to record
this number again, especially for the show. I said was this
possible? He said it would depend upon the costs, and I said well
you find out whether we can afford it, and I am asking you the
same question. But as you say the show is expensive, I don't
bloody well know what to do, except end up with a one string
banjo, and a couple of spoons and a tuba, and I'm pissed off,
because Morecambe and Wise, and Eric Sykes Shows all have big
band music.

Show No. 2.   We agree to all the swearing coming out.
Show No. 3.   The Disease Sketch, we will see in rehearsal if it's
                    too long or not.

Show No. 4.   If Tom Jackson can't do it, any member of the cast
                 who is free can.

Show No. 5.   (Page 4), We need to change from film to studio
                 because the sequence in the studio is very relevant
                 for laughs upon performer/audience relationship. If
                 we do it on film it might die the death.

                 Re Frank Bough I suggest we first try and get him,
                 and if they say no, we ask the BBC how did Angela
                 Rippon get on to the Morecambe & Wise Show. If
                 it's a matter of showing legs, Frank Bough can roll
                 his trousers up to the knees.

Show No. 6.   OK cancel hand-held camera.

Show No. 7.   (Page 6), This we need to be in the studio, at that
                 point again for laughter control. That is the actor
                 can only get it by playing to the audience live.
                 (Page 12), OK agree – use film.

                 In place of Henry Cooper use Nosher Powell or
                 any big bruiser.

Must fly, as I am off to America. Fuck everybody, why don't you
try it yourself.

As ever, yours always the noo,
Spike Milligan

Mike Harding Esq.
BBC Enterprises
Villiers House
London W5

8 *March 1978*

Dear Mike,

Thanks for your letter of the 16th February. In your opening
sentence you only repeated what I have told you in my letter to
you of the 12th February, that is 'we have only issued nine Goon
Shows in the last 20 years'. That is telling me what I just told you.
Please explain to me what you mean when you say each year your
selection gets a little more difficult. As there are about 150 Goon
Shows on tape I cannot see where the difficulty lies. If you
subtract 9 from 150 you are left with 141 shows.

   Likewise you mention having to chase up Transcription
Services. The only reason why you chase Transcription Services
is because your BBC Enterprises had no idea of the existence of
the shows already held by Transcription Services. They hold 104,
so I cannot see what the difficulty there is. I cannot believe that
you cannot afford to issue more than we do at the moment,
surely as the records make a profit, I presume, in which case you
must have covered your costs. Would you explain to me what
precisely the financial difficulty is?

   I'm only trying to find out the reason for 9 L.P.S. in 20 years.

Sincerely,
Spike Milligan

P. S. I think you ought to take me out to dinner and explain to
   me the workings of BBC Records.

Michael Grade Esq.
London Weekend Television Limited
South Bank Television Centre
London SE1

29 June 1978

Dear Michael,

MELTING POT

The BBC refused to transmit these shows, and I am not quite sure of their reason, I think it was a mixture of their fear of the Racial implications in it, and (b) it wasn't that funny.

I had a major problem with this show, the Pilot was an absolute riot, this I cast myself; however when the series was mooted the BBC insisted on casting it, and put in three actors, the like of which I wouldn't give a job scrubbing Camels arses in the desert.

However, believe me the series was funny, and it can be made hysterical if the right actors were chosen for the parts – are you interested?

As your father still owes me £25 from the Wintergardens at Eastbourne, take me to dinner at the Trattoo, and if nothing else, we can have a laugh.

I remember you as a little Spotty Herbert, about three, standing by your father's desk crying, I think he owed you £25 from Eastbourne as well.

Let me know.

Love, light and peace,
Spike Milligan

P. S. How do you make a Jewish Omelette?

Lord Bernstein, LLD
Granada Television Limited
London W1

20 June 1985

Dear Sydney,

I have had on hire a small black and white portable Sony TV.
1U.K. Set, for umpteen years, I discovered today I have paid over
£600 for it, don't you think the Company at this stage, ought to
make a gift of it to me, having paid for it five times over.

   You understand this is only an exploratory letter, because I
don't want to bring your Empire crushing down.

   Last week I was at a Brains Trust, at the Belmont Synagogue,
I was the only Christian there, and I want you to know that. I
hope your continuing ongoing purchases of Bacon's masterpieces
(do you get them at Sainsbury's) still goes on. I remember talking
to one of the Securicor men in the foyer of Granada in
Manchester, and I was discussing the painting with him, his
comments: 'he's splodged it, hasn't he', and somehow I didn't feel
as secure as I had before.

Love, light and peace,
Spike Milligan

14

Crunching the Numbers

J. Willson, Esq.
Coutts & Co.
440 Strand
London WC2

4 February 1968

Dear Mr Willson,

How dare you remind me about this trivial overdraft when my Post Office Savings have reached £17.8.0?

I must warn you that once a month I put all my overdrafts into a hat and the one that comes out first, I clear. If you are not careful, I won't even put your name in the hat but, good news Mr Willson, I have instructed Ireland not to beat Scotland when they play at Merryfield. Also I will be able to clear this overdraft by, say, the middle of May, by which time you may have even got this letter.

I will get my Manager to give you a ring and I would like very much to come and have lunch with you.

Sincerely,
Spike Milligan

Coutts & Co.
440 Strand
London WC2

29 January 1971

Dear Mr Milligan,

Spike Milligan Productions Ltd

I write with reference to the arrangements made in July last when the Bank agreed to allow a limit of overdraft of £5,000 on the Company's account for the ensuing six months. The period has now elapsed and we wish to review the arrangements in the normal course.

If you are able to visit me for lunch at the Bank I would welcome the opportunity of discussing the matter of your Company's borrowing requirements for the next six months with you.

No doubt you will telephone me beforehand in order that a mutually convenient time for your visit can be arranged.

Yours sincerely,
J. Willson
Assistant Manager

(S) Help!
(N) Its not an overdraft –
it's an arrangement

Coutts & Co.
440 Strand
London WC2

13 July 1972

Dear Mr Milligan,

I have received your letter of the 11th of this month and am grateful to you for having drawn my personal attention to the serious mistake that has been made by us concerning the Tax Reserve Certificates which we have been holding for you.

The matter has been fully investigated and it is quite clear to me from the report which I have been given that we did act most carelessly on this occasion and I am not going to make any pretences or excuses to the contrary.

I am sure that you will not wish to be bothered with the technical details of the mistake. It was, in itself, quite a simple one, but as so often can happen, it set in train a series of events leading to the present unhappy position. This, of course, will be put right, so far as it can be at the moment, by adjusting the entries made between the deposit and current accounts concerned and, needless to say, by the cancellation of the interest which has accrued on that part of the overdraft directly attributable to the events about which I write.

I do so understand how maddened you must have been by our stupidity but, as Manager of this Office, Sir, I cannot conceal from you my anxiety that, because of it, you no longer consider our services to be worthwhile. My sense of concern would indeed be deepened were it your intention – as your remarks could perhaps imply – to bring to an end our association of some years standing which we, ourselves, have looked upon with not a little pleasure.

You know, we at Coutts, would like to think that we have the 'edge' over our competitors in the quality of the service which we provide for our customers and whilst, sadly, there are still times when it is certainly not apparent, our efforts are constantly being directed to that end. This is not to say, among other things, that in time we shall be able to guarantee a faultless performance. That can never be and it would be foolish as well as misleading to suggest to you that it could.

Correspondence is all very well, of course, in serving certain necessary purposes. Nevertheless it does have its limitations and both Mr D. Osborne – the Assistant Manager most closely concerned with the day to day running of your accounts – and I, attach the very greatest importance to meeting our customers personally. In my experience, such meetings are invariably of some value but never more so than when some difficulty or problem has to be overcome. It occurs to me, therefore, should you be able to find the time, that you might like to come in to see us and if, perhaps, you would be good enough to let me know beforehand, we should be delighted if you would join us for luncheon and a tour of the Office afterwards! In the meantime I enclose the Tax Reserve Certificates for £3,443.78, as you have requested, together with a form of receipt for your signature and return.

Yours sincerely,
A. D. Southgate
Manager

A. D. Southgate Esq.
Coutts & Company
440 Strand
London WC2

3 August 1972

Dear Mr Southgate,

Thank you for your circular. I see that the lunch season is coming in, and I am willing to partake of your high table.

I would like you to bear in mind, that if the value of the lunch is over £10, I would rather you take the amount off my overdraft, and I will sign the menu, as though having partaken, of the meal.

Respectfully,
Spike Milligan
Coutts Victim
Nervous Breakdown
Ward 3
Middlesex

———◆———

The Rt. Hon. Denis Healey MP
Treasury Chambers
London SW1

5 September 1975

Dear Mr Healey,

It was nice of you to have taken time off to have written me such a long letter, I appreciate all the contents and explanations. But, my Manager is still downstairs working out VAT forms as she has been for the last three hours, and 'there's the rub', and whilst on the subject of Shakespeare, when it comes to VAT might I suggest 'a good idea should give way to a better one'.

Anyhow, thank you again for replying.

Sincerely,
Spike Milligan

P. S. Don't bother to reply to this letter, I know you are very
busy – if you are not you should be.

———•———

J. F. Prideaux Esq. OBE
National Westminster Bank Limited
41 Lothbury
London EC2

4 September 1972

Dear Mr Prideaux,

Thank you for your letter; even accepting all the excuses I fail to see how you can claim to have a cable system, when money sent from Jersey on Friday 28th July, was still in England on 1st August at mid-day, during which time, in desperation I telephoned the jokers at Barclays Bank in London who told me the money was in Bristol, I phoned Mrs Boyd in Bristol at mid-day and she told me the money was with Mr Poole in London. No amount of excuses will change the quality of this as being other than gross inefficiency, I would go further – chaos.

I am afraid on the strength of this I am writing to the Financial Times, otherwise some other poor joker will be getting the same treatment.

Alas, I am not the sort of person that can keep quiet about this sort of thing.

Respectfully,
Spike Milligan
Dictated by Spike Milligan and signed in his absence

———•———

National Westminster Bank Limited
41 Lothbury
London EC2

5 September 1972

Dear Mr Milligan,

I am writing in reply to your recent letter addressed to the Chairman and whilst there is little I can add to Mr Prideaux's letter of 7th August, I regret that you do not feel able to accept our apologies.

Yours sincerely,
S. Wild
Director and General Manager

———•———

Mr S. Wild
Director and General Manager
National Westminster Bank Limited
41 Lothbury
London EC2

13 September 1972

Dear Mr Wild,

I do accept your apology. I am not ungallant in that respect. The only thing I cannot accept is a mistake repeated twice to the detriment of the customer which caused me a lot of unnecessary outlay of money. Being a human being I naturally suffered remorse as a result of this, wouldn't you?

I mean the banks have lost nothing but I have, and if I owned the bank I would make a thorough investigation of this system to see if it could be improved – I don't suppose this has been done.

No I am a human being but I just cannot accept inefficiency.

Yours sincerely,
Spike Milligan

⎯⎯⎯●⎯⎯⎯

J. M. Bankier Esq
DHSS
North Fylde
War Pensions
Blackpool FY5 3TA

19 February 1988

Dear Mr Bankier (The rubber stamp Controller),

I am in receipt of your communication in which you informed me that you have paid £8 into my bank account.

I have written to the Queen and she is going to make it a national day of rejoicing.

Please let me know when this happens again because the contents of the bank are rather insecure, it is the Midland Bank at Barnet, and the only bank that has a begging bowl outside the front door.

Warm Regards,
Spike Milligan

Ⓢ What the hell is all this about? Ⓝ

———◆———

*ALL THIS LUNACY —
FOR A MORTGAGE — IM THE
END I COULD'NT STAND THE
CHAOS- SO I CANCELLED. 1974
AND PAID CASH FOR
THE HOUSE*

Palme Court,
LONDON. W. 2.

1974

The Managing Director,
National Post Office Building Society,
Waterloo House,
High Street,
Epsom,
Surrey.

Dear Sir,

ACCOUNT NO. L. 36062.

Re the mortgage I was applying for through Mr. Desmond Finnan,
I now no longer wish to proceed with it.

I find it is taking far too long and it is far too complex.

                    Respectfully,

                    Spike Milligan.

*[He wanted to buy a flat for one of his children. Spike and forms are not
good bedfellows. It really did turn into chaos.]*

PART FOUR
Words of Support

15

Man of the People

Christian Simpson, Esq.
BBC Television Centre
London W12

16 January 1957

Dear Christian,

I am sending you the films I spoke to you about, made by a young man called Kenneth Russell.

I realise these are not the greatest ever made, but considering the conditions he worked under, using only a cheap camera, with no-one to write the story for him, I think they show a lot of promise.

I would be grateful if you would bear him in mind in the future in case you may be able to use him as I think he deserves a helping hand.

Sincerely,
Spike Milligan

———◆———

Charles Chilton Esq.
BBC
Aeolian Hall
London W1

10 November 1965

Dear Charles,

I really have been so much overworked in the last month, that I haven't had a chance to even think about writing another script. Could you ask them to be kind and hold their horses until the New Year?

I think the next one will be for the police, as at least they are very much underentertained and very deserving of a night's entertainment gratis.

Regarding the Navy Show whereas being there was wonderful and the lunch and the painted hall were all very wonderful, once again we suffered with this dreadful malaise of snobs and their wives and hangers on being in the audience, and not understanding a word of what was being spoken. I am going to have to make a stand this time, I really must say if when we arrive at the police show it is populated by thousands of people who really aren't of the force other than by marriage then I am going to walk out. I am sorry to be like this, I am not really wanting to rock the boat, it's just that I do think the rank and file ought to get preference here because all the top brass have the money to go out to big shows whenever they feel like it, the whole idea of these shows was to get people like privates, ratings and the lower echelons of the services to a free entertainment, up to now this has not happened and consequently we are really not getting a very good reception to the shows. I really think the BBC ought to do something about it, because the whole series has become a mockery.

Anyhow that's how I feel and I am sure you would rather know how I feel than how I didn't. Apart from that I did enjoy being at Greenwich, it was wonderful being there.

Paddy is at the moment still in hospital with this advance pregnancy sickness, and she was heartbroken at having to turn down what for her was the start of a new career in sound radio. However, she will write to you when she is better in hopes of perhaps doing something in the future.

My regards to you all, life is hell, what's your excuse?

Spike Milligan

Sydney Bernstein, Esq.
Granada Television Limited
London W1

26 October 1966

Dear Sydney Bernstein,

This is just a try on. I am trying to organise a green room for the artists at the Mermaid Theatre, and was wondering if an exchange for a plug every night on the show, you would like to loan us a television set for the stage staff and the artists to enjoy when they are not actually working.

If you do not acquiesce to this threat, I shall have to have words with Harold Wilson to put pressure on you, who might easily transfer you to the Conservative Birthday Honours List.

Anyhow,

Regards,
As ever,
Spike Milligan

Roy Jenkins, Esq.
Home Secretary
Home Office
London SW1

20 December 1966

Dear Roy Jenkins,

This is a plea at Christmas to try and help quash a prison sentence for someone who has broken their probation, his name is Ian Hewitson.

He has been, and still is a schizophrenic, constantly under treatment from drugs, and as if this is not enough burden for one man to carry, he is also a homosexual. He has been appearing in my play The Bed Sitting Room at the Mermaid Theatre; at all times he is so kind and sensitive and always willing to do the right thing.

I feel even though he has broken the law his mental suffering is so great that it in itself is a life sentence. If what he tells me is true, he spent a night with a 20 year old boy/man at a hotel, but apparently the mother of the boy/man in question said that he only had the mentality of a child of ten.

Ian Hewitson was put on probation but apparently he has broken this and must go into prison. I wonder as today the homosexual bill (Mr Leo Abse) has been passed unopposed, can you possibly see your way to easing the sentence for the man in question.

I will be willing to stand bail and I am sure that he would not break it if he knew it was me standing bail for him.

You can always contact me at my office at 9 Orme Court, London W2. Phone No. PAR 1544.

I have never written to a Home Secretary before, so I might as well take the opportunity of wishing you a Merry Christmas.

Respectfully,
Spike Milligan

M. F. Cunningham Esq.
Mechanical Copyright Society Ltd.
London S W 16

5 May 1969

Dear Mr Cunningham,

With reference to your letter of the 30th April, Mr Edgington is talking rubbish, he actually wrote the music for NING NANG NONG. I myself certainly cannot accept the fee for the work of the composer, and it would be wrong.

He is a very simple man and does not want to be bothered with filling in forms, and office work.

I have spoken to him and told him he will have to accept money for his compositions, and I have offered to fill in the forms for him, and he has agreed to accept the money.

Will you please find enclosed a fresh form for NING NANG NONG agreed by him and me. If you will forward all the monies to this office I will make the payment to him. This will simplify things and make life easier for everyone.

Would you please let me know if this is all acceptable.

Sincerely,
Spike Milligan

The Rt. Hon. William Whitelaw MC MP
Secretary of State for Northern Ireland
68 Whitehall
London SW1

29 March 1972

Dear Mr Whitelaw,

I recently wrote a letter to the Stormont Government, with no political motives in mind, requesting permission to go to Long Kesh Internment Camp to entertain the internees.

They understandably refused me, but in the new consideration of phasing out the internees of Long Kesh, it might make pleasant publicity with the new attitude in Ulster, and I would be able to come most any time that was suitable to the authorities concerned.

I must emphasise I am not doing this for personal publicity, but I think it would be good for the whole new vista being set up in Ulster.

I do hope you allow me this privilege.

Respectfully,
Spike Milligan

GOVERNMENT HOUSE,

HILLSBOROUGH,

NORTHERN IRELAND

2nd April, 1972.

Dear Mr Milligan

Thank you so much for your letter
of 29th March and your idea of going to
Long Kesh Internment Camp to entertain
the internees.

In the delicate situation which
there is here at present I am sure you
will understand if I say that I doubt
if this is the right time for this to
happen under my auspices, but I will most
certainly bear your offer in mind for the
future.

Yours sincerely

Willie Whitelaw

Spike Milligan, Esq.,
9 Orme Court,
LONDON, W.2.

The Rt. Hon. William Whitelaw MC, MP
Government House
Hillsborough
Northern Ireland

5 April 1972

Dear Mr Whitelaw,

Thank you for your letter. I understand the situation. However, can you still help me?

I received an anonymous Christmas card from one of the internees at Long Kesh, and in some way I would like to reply and thank them for sending it to me. Is there a notice board which the internees read, on which the attached letter could be pinned.

Thanking you in anticipation.

Love, light and peace,
Spike Milligan

Long Kesh Internment Camp

5 April 1972

Dear Lads,

I received an anonymous Christmas card from Long Kesh, and this note is to thank whoever it was for that card, and give my belated Christmas greetings.

Love, light and peace,
Spike Milligan

Nikolai Lunkov Esq.
The Russian Embassy
London W8

20 January 1975

Your Excellency,

As a socialist, and an extreme left wing socialist, I do find that the Soviet Union's attitude to the Jewish Community in Russia rather unhealthy. Basically, there is no point in retaining somebody who does not wish to belong to the Russian community. It is economically, politically and humanitarianally much better to (a) deport them or, (b) emigrate. To retain them in prison also is ill received in the world press at large. I do hope you might consider the importance of what I say, and I mean it not only in the best interests of Russian Jews, but also in the best interests of Russian society themselves.

Sincerely,
Spike Milligan

Harold Evans Esq.
Sunday Times

25 April 1978

Dear Harold,

I would like you to know that I support you totally in your
magnificent and highly moral fight. To uphold certain principles,
which in essence are the voice of truth, and it's high time that
such effort was made. To penetrate this medieval wall of
hypocrisy and quasi truths and half moralities which are really so
archaic that the people who support them (this case the House of
Lords) are totally out of touch with the essential quality which
makes man the one creature that can reach out for the perfect
truth.

If in any way I can help, do let me know.

Again I send you my warm regards for this splendid fight.

Love, light and peace,
Spike Milligan

———————————

The Sunday Times
200 Gray's Inn Road
London WC1

2 May 1979

Dear Spike,

God bless you for your quick and perceptive response to what
happened in Strasbourg. If the opportunity is seized it is a
tremendous chance to let more light into the dark corners of this

country. The English judge who voted against us is, incidentally, the man who not only thought that caning was okay but said that when he was at school he enjoyed it. Never mind. The Italians, Cypriots and Germans and other despised races came to our rescue.

All that is required now is somebody to wave a magic wand and get the Management and the Unions to agree to print our paper.

Regards,
Harold Evans
Editor

Ken Livingstone Esq.
GLC
Leader of the Council
County Hall
London SE1

16 June 1983

Dear Ken,

Whilst I was away I had a telegram from Anthony Graham saying that Coombe Cliff was safe.

If you were involved in this, along with Tony Banks, would you please pass on my thanks, and also for tolerating all the insults.

Love, light and peace,
Spike Milligan

P. S. So they didn't blow you up when you went there.

Peter Cookson Esq.

4 March 1982

Dear Master Carpenter,

I have received your bill for two million pounds for putting the shelf in the carsey. I did find this a bit steep, not the bill, but the angle of the shelf. So, I will be going to the International Lending Fund to raise the two million to pay for this job.

In the meantime, I'm sending you £80, not £70, as you asked, but £10 will cover inflation while the money is in transit.

I will be considering your charges for leaping on and off walls, drinking tea, and being attacked by the house cat.

You will be hearing from my Solicitor in the morning, which is more than I bloody well do.

I am keeping your letter because it's so funny.

As ever,
Spike Milligan

[The reason the master carpenter's letter is not here – Spike really did keep it.]

Alan Edwards Esq.
Barclays Bank plc
95 Queensway
London W2

2 November 1983

Dear Alan,

I hear, via Norma that one of the 4½ million unemployed has broken into your bank, and of all things, stole the money, and left the furniture.

Find enclosed £1. sterling to start things off again.

Sincerely,
Spike Milligan

———•◦•———

Jim Slater Esq.
General Secretary
National Union of Seamen
London SW4

9 November 1983

Dear Jim,

Just to thank you and all your men for your enlightened attitude towards the dumping of waste in the seas. I do not see why working class men's organisations should not be involved at every level; it's their environment.

In Australia Jack Mundy, who was head of the Builders Union actually took part in conservation by banning any building from being pulled down by his organisation Greenbelt. Large areas of Sydney and Australia were saved thanks to that workers union.

Alas that movement has gone into decline, but I was just pointing out that working class socialism should be in the forefront of all matters concerning their own country, and areas of the world that are pertinent to it.

Love, light and peace,
Spike Milligan

———————

Gareth Gwenlan Esq.
British Broadcasting Corporation
Television Centre
London W12

10 April 1984

Dear Gareth,

I thought, as you have nothing to do, the enclosed might help.

Love, light and peace,
Spike Milligan

[He sent Gareth a box of Britain's soldiers. The scene shifters were on strike. There were pickets outside the BBC.]

———————

British Broadcasting Corporation
Television Centre
London W12

10 April 1984

Dear Spike,

I have sent half the soldiers out to the main gate to sort out the pickets. I have given the other half red jerseys in order to give them training for next season.

Thank you for your kind gift.

Gareth Gwenlan

———◆———

The Editor
Guardian

18 June 1985

Dear Sir,

This letter is not for publication, it's just to say that amid all the blood of football, and the agony of hijackers, what a sheer delight to see the photograph of PC Adams enjoying a lunchtime treat while guarding the test wicket.

It brought a great amount of light into my day.

Sincerely,
Spike Milligan

———◆———

Richard Hearsey Esq.
London Weekend Television Limited
South Bank Television Centre
London SE1

1 July 1986

Dear Richard,

How extremely kind and compassionate of you to send me two bottles of anaesthetic. Having found a soft touch at last I will be informing you of all my future illnesses as and when they arrive.

Again, thank you so very much.

Love, light and peace,
Spike Milligan

———————— • ————————

The Editor
Grimsby Evening Telegraph

17 May 1988

Dear Sir,

I was watching a programme on BBC2 on the Grimsby fishing industry, and I could not but say, after I had seen it, how much I was in admiration of those men involved in the fishing trade in Grimsby.

It is a pity the government is not as anxious to pump money into this industry as in British Leyland and other companies who seem to constantly lose money.

Sincerely,
Spike Milligan

———————— • ————————

The Editor
Jewish Chronicle

26 July 1989

Dear Sir,

I cannot but comment on the bureaucratic indifference and in many cases inhuman reaction to the cause of identifying War Criminals in England. I resent a Government that out of tax payer's money commissioned people to investigate a case to be made against Nazi crimes. A long investigation takes place, the report states categorically that the crimes committed by these men, not against one person or against thousands, but millions, shows enough evidence for these men to go before a Court of Law. The moment it comes out The Labour Party says 'It is too late. They won't be able to get witnesses from Russia or Estonia. Forget it.' Likewise, the Home Office, who were instrumental in commissioning the report then start to say 'Oh no, we still can't bring them to justice – we have to ask Parliament.' To put it plain this system is arse about face. Why didn't they ask Parliament first, whether if evidence were brought to show they should be brought to justice, and on the strength of the yeas or nays, *then* to proceed before spending the tax payer's money and that would be a positive project. No, it is all open to any amount of odds.

I think that those concerned with this wishy washy thinking should have spent six months in Auchwitz. I think it would have done them good.

Yours faithfully,
Spike Milligan
Baffled Tax Payer

M. Ruzek (His Excellency. Czech. Ambassador.)

Dear Excellency,

I am an Irishman, whose country fought a long bitter struggle
for freedom, and so I speak with understanding of the sorrowful
state of your own people. But, in the darkness let me point to
small shafts of hopeful lights that are starting and have
started to glow.

First, the fact that Czechoslovakia, is spiritually as a nation
undefeated! By your restraint in the face of prompted Russian
violence, you have turned their military occupation into an
empty victory, to the watching world, there was nothing so
comic, as Russian tanks, bristling with guns and aggression, with
nothing to fight! It was like a lion tamer, cracking his whip in an
empty cage. They were praying that you would take up arms, so
they could have (like Hungary) a blood bath, while they said
'See, we have proved that they were Fascist reactionaries'?
Instead, they were surrounded by unarmed peaceful citizens,
mothers with babies, young students with flowers, all asking
'Why have you invaded us' – and not one Russian could give an
answer. What a victory you had against violence, the first since
Gandhi and his non-violence started the undermining of then
the most powerful nation on earth. England, without firing a
shot. Today, England is in decline, and India starting to grow.
Again, the occupation has split the Communist World, that in
itself has weakened Russia, and Russia herself has made enemies
she never had before, and among *Communist* Countries and
Parties everywhere – in France, Italy and others as you know.
The sacrifice of Jan Palach set alight not only his funeral torch, he
made a light that will never go out, and a pall of smoke that will
however eternally over those men in Russia on whose head it will
rest for eternity.

So take heart, restraint, faith, courage must and *will* one day,
destroy the aggressor – with patience – time will remove him

physically, even though you may not believe in God, these words from the bible have strength 'When the strong have devoured each other, the meek will inherit the earth.'

My regards and love to you and your people,
Spike Milligan

———•———

Ron Todd Esq.
General Secretary
TGWU
London SW1

2 August 1989

Dear Ron,

I would just like to say I sympathise with you and what I think is very pernicious background moves by the Dock Authority, to whittle away through emotional and financial blackmail at your dockers.

I think you are going to have to give in to the current situation, but I do think you might have to have a total new rethink as to how to go about it in future to avoid the dockers being picked off by the Dock Authority.

Anyhow, I know my letter doesn't help, but I just wanted to let you know I support your cause.

If there is anything I can do to help, please let me know and if I can I will.

Sincerely,
Spike Milligan

———•———

Ms Janet Paraskeva
England Director
National Lotteries Charities Board
London WC2

8 April 1997

Dear Janet,

Begging letter number one million. I am Vice President of the
Rye Rugby Club and to put it bluntly they are skint and
desperately in need of funds. We have no grand stand or facilities
for showers, changing rooms etc etc.

    £3 millions would do or something approaching it.

Sincerely,
Spike Milligan
Bankruptcy number – 672

———•—•———

The Editor
The Daily Mirror

6 March 1998

Dear Sir,

Last Christmas I tried to get some underprivileged children to come
and stay with my wife and me for Christmas with lunch, presents
and to spend Christmas week with us. However, out of a nation of
over fifty-five million people, I was unable to make this happen.

Sincerely,
Spike Milligan

16

Mental Health

Charles Denton Esq.
British Broadcasting Corporation
Television Centre
London W12

14 June 1967

Dear Charles Denton,

Your offer about a person being concerned with some situation or place does appeal to me, because the place I am concerned about is the world and the person homosapiens.

Love to meet you for a drink because I am literally bursting apart at the seams with grief at the Christian world as it is in relationship to what it should be and even sadder what it was.

My particular concern is people with mental illness being a victim myself I can speak with great authority on this subject.

Anyhow, if you get your secretary to ring mine on PAR 2768 to arrange a meeting we can have a drink together.

Regards,
Spike Milligan
Dictated by Spike Milligan and signed in his absence

[Charles had asked Spike to meet him to discuss a future programme on the state of the world.]

Miss Jan Black
Rag Committee, 1969
Gloucestershire College of Education

29 November 1968

Dear Editor,

You say your Mag is in aid of mental health! Dear Miss, there's no such thing, if there was anybody in position of power with any semblance of mental health, do you think the world would be in this bloody mess. Young minds at risk is different. – Anybody with a young mind is taking a risk – young means fresh – unsullied, ready to be gobbled up in an adult world, bringing the young into a visionless world of adults, like all our leaders. Their world is dead – dead – dead, and my God, that's why it stinks! They look at youth in horror – and say 'They are having a revolution', but what do they want. I say they don't know what they want, but they know what they don't want, and that is, the repetition of the past mistakes, towards which the adult old order is still heading. War – armistice – building up the pre war standards – capitalism – labour – crisis – war and so on. I digress.

Mental Health. I have had five nervous breakdowns, and all the medics gave me was medicine – tablets – but no love or any attempt at involvement, in this respect I might as well have been a fish in a bowl. The mentally ill need LOVE, UNDERSTANDING, TOLERANCE, as yet unobtainable on the NHS or the private world of psychiatry but tablets yes, and a bill for £5. 5s. 0d. a visit – if they know who you are, it's £10. 10s. 0d. a visit – the increased fee has an immediate depressing effect, so you come out worse than you went in.

As yet, I have not been cured, patched up via chemicals, yes.
Letter unfinished, but I've run out of time, sorry.

Regards,
Spike Milligan

Father Michael Gibbons
St Colman's
Inishbofin
Co. Galway

18 March 1968

Dear Father Gibbons,

Thank you for your offer of a sanctuary. Having had so many so called Christian Monasteries turned down direct requests for help in allowing me to overcome my mental problems, they immediately refer me to the National Health service.

I believe in Jesus, and I find that Christianity has almost forgotten him.

This Nashdon Abbey (I think that's the name and how you spell it) with central heating, no travel problems, having to travel on packed tubes – a nice warm cosy situation, in fact, 'cut-off' from Christian Society.

There is a lot of re-thinking to be done on a massive scale, from the Pope downwards, before that simple Christian message of 'Go ye among them' comes back again.

I possibly will come and see you one day, you sound a nice person, and that's how we start being Christian.

As ever,
Spike Milligan

Major-General C. M. F. Deakin CB, CBE
Mental Health Research Fund
London W1

26 April 1968

Dear Major-General Deakin,

Your letter of the 11th April to hand. Strange you should write to me because I don't know whether you know I myself am a victim of mental ill health. In fact sometimes I find it very difficult to carry on.

But what is difficult is the complete lack of understanding by people in mental homes, and I mean, doctors, matrons and nurses, who seem to have absolutely no idea of what emotional understanding they should adopt to gain the confidence of the patient.

At the present moment mental health means one thing only, and that is giving the sufferer drugs; this is not difficult, I could buy the drugs and administer them myself, but as I say there is *no* understanding of the actual emotional needs.

In fact, my friend actor and writer, Barry Humphries likewise suffers in the same way as I do, in fact, at the time of writing he is in Beech Hill Nursing home, North London, and I am about to go into Bowden House Clinic, Harrow on the Hill. Both Humphries and myself are agreed that the attitudes of nurses and staff to patients is terrifying; not because the staff are heartless, it is just that nobody has instructed them in the actual needs of the patient, that is apart from giving them medicine. Barry Humphries and I have agreed to write a white paper explaining where the doctors etc. fall down. There is one thing I will point out right from the start, you don't smile when you go into a mental sufferers room, it looks exactly the same as someone smiling at a funeral.

Anyhow, by all means let us meet, perhaps you would care to have lunch with me and we can talk about the charity side then. I don't feel much disposed to charity at the moment, as I am about to pay 53 gns. a week to go into a home where, in fact, all you really get are tranquilisers. I will get my manager Norma Farnes to contact you after I have pulled out of the present depression.

Sincerely,
Spike Milligan
Dictated by Spike Milligan over the
telephone and signed in his absence

Miss Marjorie ▮▮▮
Kent

18 June 1968

Dear Marjorie ▮▮▮,

You will drop dead when you discover I am answering your letter of the 12th March, 1966. I may have answered it already, if I have then I will stop writing immediately.

I did enjoy your letter, and understood all the contents and meanings, and I enjoyed the poetry very much, despite the remark that the editor had pruned one of the pieces.

It's all very painful and hopeless, isn't it. What can you do, you just go on living.

If ever you are in London, and would like a drink or something like that, or perhaps you would like to be hit with an iron club, let me know.

Anyhow, I am always willing to see people, and talk to them there is little else one can do.

Sincerely,
Spike Milligan

Mr Christopher Mayhew, MP for Woolwich East
Chairman
National Association for Mental Health
c/o House of Commons

14 October 1970

Dear Mr Christopher Mayhew,

I can only compliment you on your concern for the mentally ill. Having been a victim of mental illness since the war, and having been in and out of what are laughingly called psychiatric establishments, I am only too well aware of the lack of understanding and love between doctors, nurses and patients. I mention the word 'love' because it is an essential ingredient for the recovery of the mental patient, and whereas medics will prescribe drugs there is absolutely no attempt to offer what is the greatest remedy of all, that is, love and understanding.

Of course, secondly, as you say, the almost complete indifference in the election manifestos to this problem of mental illness makes it necessary for a man like yourself to take action. If there is anything I can do to help please let me know. Perhaps you might like to take lunch with me some day and you can hear from a mentally ill person where the shortcomings lie. Believe me, if you haven't suffered mentally you can never really understand the problem – it is like a language, you have to know it to understand.

I do as much work as I can for various mental illness organisations. If I can help you, you just have to say the word.

I saw written on a wall in Finchley 'Psychiatry Kills'. Very strange words, but it had an essence of truth in it.

Love, light and peace,
Spike Milligan

[One of literally hundreds of letters Spike received from the general public with mental health issues. This was his answer.]

Philip ███████ *Esq.*
London E2

8 *June 1971*

Dear Philip,

Just write your troubles on a piece of paper and see if I can help. This is because you can't get through on the 'phone I have been away filming and I am filming off and on until the middle of June.

Okay – write.

Love, light and peace,
Spike

———◆———

Philip ███████ *Esq.*
London E2

21 *June 1971*

Dear ███,

Thank you for your letter. I am sorry I am so busy.

I do not misunderstand you at all and do not be afraid to write to me because I am only too willing to help people who are having trouble, especially young people like yourself. I think you are a splendid person, ███, and I would be proud to have you as a son, so don't let people say anything to the contrary.

You keep on trying your way with music. Remember there are also musics outside of the pop world, for instance Ravel and Debussy wrote exquisite music even though it's not electronic. It is electrifying to those who like it.

Like you say, words never sound the same on paper, but don't worry just write when you feel like it and I will try and see you if and when I can, but right now I really am a busy man.

Love, light and peace,
Spike

———◆———

████████ *Esq.*
Cornwall

13 February 1973

My dear ████,

I got your letter and one does not have to read more than a few lines to realise that you are going through it. It's a cross you have to bear, ████, nobody is quite to blame for people like us getting ill, it's just that you were born with a great emotional range, and of course after such a panorama, your emotions are terribly naked and vulnerable in areas that other people do not possess.

You *will* get better because you have got fire inside. Try doing what I do, try and enjoy the fact that you are having a breakdown in your own miserable way, and think that you have not got any work to do, and at the same time you are getting paid for it. It may not make you feel better, but at least you will know that you and your wife are provided for during your illness.

Of course I understand it only too well, but as for trying to *explain* it, you know, as I do, it is impossible, and yet the damn thing is so positive. If it is any help ████. I do know, whom

I consider, a good psychiatrist, but bearing in mind that nobody can ever quite cure this illness, but there are psychiatrists who can alleviate it to a degree.

I know the BBC can be terribly wearing, because there is no such person as BBC consequently it has no heart, and the people who live in such an organisation either accept the status of being entirely unemotional or people like yourself who fight the inertia which comes with such an organisation. What makes me sick about all this is I don't suppose for one moment Charles Curran even knows that you are not working, now how can you expect a firm to be run with heart if the man who runs it does not know what is going on in the lower echelons. But don't carry any malice or hatred ▓, that only makes you burn faster and the heat is unbearable.

If I had the time I would come down and see you for a while but alas I can't.

I notice you are staying at ▓▓▓▓▓▓▓▓▓▓▓▓▓▓▓▓. Is this the home of ▓▓▓▓▓▓▓▓ the painter, I am almost certain he lives there and he is a friend of mine and a very splendid man whom I met in the war in Italy. If so, please make it known to him he seems to be a very kind man.

I hope that you are being given some kind of sedative or tranquilisers, because just to send you away is just transferring the illness to a new geographical location.

I won't write further ▓, because I think you know that I understand your feelings and how your mind must be searching at the moment to find out if you should take a new angle on life, and suchlike, but it will be the same old life when you get better and it will go on and on and on, and you just have to get used to it Chum.

I am feeling for you.

Love, light and peace,
Spike Milligan

[This is Spike at his best. Compassion was his saving grace.]

Elizabeth ████████████,
Norfolk

27 July 1973

Dear Elizabeth,

Thank you for your letter. I like you am a neurotic. Don't worry too much about only having three 'A' Levels, I never passed any exams at all. You don't tell me how old you are, I presume you are a young woman, and I suppose so do you. I have no idea what to do about mental illness, I am still in the dark, I still live a gloomy life but I have to press on to provide for my wife and four children. There are literally a million or two million people like us, and what you have got to do is to get used to the fact that you will go up and down in life and try and get used to the fact, that does help a bit. There are some drugs which do help, but do not cure. The most important thing to avoid is habit-forming sleeping pills.

I wish I could help you more. Next stop God.

Love, light and peace,
Spike Milligan

Edward ▮▮▮ *Esq.*
Middlesex

22 September 1976

Dear Edward,

Your letter is one of a slow trickle of such incidents, what's happened to you, and in other people's lives.

It's unbelievable, but then John Profumo was a classical case of what current morality can do, that is, because of Profumo's sex life he was dismissed from the Foreign Office, where apparently he was one of the most brilliant men in office of this century. What this system is saying is, we have a man here who has a cure for cancer, but because he had sexual intercourse, hanging from a gas bracket, with a prostitute, we do not wish to know the cure for cancer. In your case they don't even have any immorality to go on to discharge you, but they are willing to put you out to grass because you have an illness, an illness in fact which does not incapacitate your ability to teach, which makes it even more perverse.

But then, this is the society that we are living in, a very hard, thick, tasteless, plastic, self-indulgent *mob*.

We are isolated (that is you and I, and our kind), and the mob rushes around us because it says that we are different, in fact, in a strange way, King Louis and Marie Antoinette, through no choice of their own found themselves King and Queen of France, and the mob didn't like it – alas the mob that doesn't like us *runs* the country, and there is no way out for us except to commiserate with each other; and strangely by this isolation I feel myself more a Prince than a figure of scorn.

Yes, do send me a book of your poetry, I am sending you one of mine.

Love, light and peace,
Spike Milligan

Andrew
London W5

19 August 1977

Dear Andrew,

Briefly, I still suffer with depression, they started in about 1953, and the smallest action or word by someone can bring it on again. However, I have come to the conclusion that one has to live with it, it's best to take this approach, and I am certain I am right. If one is born with one leg shorter than the other, no drug in the world is going to make it grow any longer, so say to yourself OK I am stuck with it.

Now, good news, I have got much better at being able to accept it in the last five years, and they are not as frequent as they used to be, and I realise that if it happens they will pass off, like any other illness.

I realise the Hell of it, but that's what life is all about. I have been on all the drugs, but now I do not take any, except 10 mg. Triptozole at night, which I am also gradually reducing to 5 mg. I don't know if any of the drugs ever did me any harm, as I am still physically very fit, but I have no idea what effect they have upon the mind, other than in my case, to make it very dull and sleepy.

As to a Faith Healer, I have no idea whether they work or not, as you are writing to me eight months after you have been attending a Faith Healer, I presume that it was a waste of time, and I have always suspected that it has just been the hope that is imbibed in Faith Healing that gives one a sense of relief, but then at the end of the Faith treatment, you are back to square one.

If you feel a definite benefit from any of the drugs, then my advice is to maintain taking them. Each person is chemically different, and therefore each drug acts differently, on each person, the only thing is to try them all in turn, and see which one acts best on you, though I must say I have met people on drugs who are still depressed . . .

I have had ECT, when I came to, I just cried and cried and cried, I feel that it might have broken the tension in my head, but then so would being thrown into the River, and half drowning, it's the same shock effect.

It boils down to ECT is making you have an accident under anaesthetics, it didn't do me any harm.

As for going self-employed, that is the best idea of all. I needless to say am self-employed, but even then there comes times when a whole series, proposed by the BBC, has to be cancelled because of mental illness. It is, as I say, a burden one has to carry. This way, one can handle the whole thing much better.

Love, light and peace,
Spike Milligan

Dr John Reid
Minister of State for Armed Forces
Ministry of Defence
London S W1

18 July 1997

Dear Doctor Reid,

A letter from the Prime Minister tells me that you are in fact again planning to look at the issue of British soldiers executed for offences other than murder and mutiny.

I myself would have been one of these as in World War Two I was serving as a bombadier on a gun firing on Cassino when unexpectedly the gun position was bombed by US planes killing many of us and the effect on me was debilitating. I didn't want to go on I reported sick, by which time I was stammering very badly,

I was seen by a psychiatrist who told me I was suffering from battle fatigue. In World War One I would have been considered a coward. Fortunately medicine has marched forward since shooting one's own men to 'straighten the line'. I was sent to hospital and given treatment for men like me I was given deep narcosis and this consisted of putting the patient to sleep for ten days. When this was done I felt much better but the psychiatrist told me I could 'never go back to the regiment as I might be unreliable'.

I am telling you all this because in fact these soldiers shot for cowardice were in fact suffering from battle fatigue, some people don't accept it. General Patton slapped the face of a soldier simply because he wasn't apparently wounded in the classic military way.

On the strength of what I have told you I think you ought to give a free pardon for all those men who found that they could not just 'go on'.

I do hope this letter will facilitate you that these men were harmless but not made of the right stuff as they say. I was one of them.

Sincerely,
Bombadier Milligan 94024
19th Battery Heavy Regiment

————◆————

The Editor
Daily Mail

17 March 1998

Dear Sir,

Like you I was horrified at the intention not to give posthumous pardons to those soldiers who were shot in World War 1. I have written to the Minister of Defence telling him, as I am telling you, that in World War 1 I would have been shot, because after eight months of combat I broke down in battle this time they did not shoot me they treated me for what they called Battle Fatigue.

If they had shot me the world would never have had the Goon Shows or any of my books and I wonder how much talent was latent in those men who were shot and died in World War 1.

Please God they will reverse this very stubborn stupid decision. In passing I would like to mention that during the war I was mentioned in Dispatches.

Sincerely,
Spike Milligan

[Spike hurting.]

17

Love, Light and Peace

November 28th

Dear Spike and Company,

Thank you for your very
kind note of good wishes to me,
and the other to the Company. (When
they go on the notice board, everyone gets
a thrill of pleasure being remembered,
but we all leave it to someone else
to write!)

We make improvements every day, and
it is getting easier and smoother, we

are almost ready to prepare ourselves
for sacrifice next week in London.
The signature Sir Tyrone puzzled
me, would it be Tony Guthrie?
Thanks a million to you all, for
thinking of us.
                Yours very sincerely
                        Flora Robson
" The Poor Man's Royal Ibsen Company "

ANTHONY WEDGWOOD BENN

20 12 6 4

Dear Spike:

Tonight's show was
the greatest. All Benns
big + small enjoyed it
to the full + none can
recall so delightful an
evening.

Tony

—

Darling — you were wonderful —
and we're sorry you went off before
we had a chance to tell
you so.

P.T.O

It was great

[signature]

Fab!!!!!!!

[signature]

It was the best show I've ever seen

Melissa

I liked it because the jokes were so funny' JOSHUA BENA

Thames Television
London WC2

5 February 1969

My Dear Spike,

I was very sorry to read in an Irish paper that your Dad has gone
to his rest. I suppose it is some little comfort that you saw him so
recently. My sympathy to you.

Eamonn Andrews

———•———

Eamonn Andrews Esq.
Thames Television
London WC2

6 February 1969

Dear Eamonn,

Thank you for your letter. Yes, he had a great life though and he
died without any pain, so it wasn't that hard. Anyhow, thanks
again.

I must come and ruin another one of your programmes
sometime. I am specialising in this gradual destruction of
television.

Hope all is well with you.

As ever,
Spike Milligan

———•———

Anthony Greenwood Esq.
Minister of Housing & Local Government
London SW1

28 February 1969

Dear Tony,

It is great to have a Minister of the Crown send me a hand written letter.

Despite all the shouting and yelling I think the present Government is bloody good; whoever I write to, even Harold Wilson he always answers the letters right away, and in this time restricted world I can't tell you how good it makes me feel to think that our Government are not just politicians, but also human beings.

I think that the Government is winning its battle with the money problem, the last trades figures were very good.

Of course, the banks who are basically non-political and obsessed with personal profit really deserve the 8% bank rate.

I am glad you liked the painting, I don't know how I do these things, I certainly can't take any credit because I don't find it difficult, so I suppose God makes people to do things to bring pleasure to his fellow men.

I am dictating this letter over the phone, because I am in bed with Chinese flu, or Japanese lurgy, otherwise I would have written this by hand.

Thank you very much, once again, and my very best wishes to you and your family.

As ever, semi loyal Socialist,
Spike Milligan
Dictated by Spike Milligan and signed in his absence

Spike starts fund for fire hero who died

By ARLISS RHIND

COMEDIAN Spike Milligan last night started a fund as a memorial to a council dustman he met only once.

That meeting was in the ward of a London hospital a few days ago where 34-year-old Edward "Ted" Ayres lay critically ill after what Spike yesterday called "an immense deed of heroism."

Mr. Ayres had been pulled, unconscious and badly burned, from a house in North Kensington, last Thursday after trying to rescue five little children during a blaze. He died at the weekend, leaving his widow Barbara, and a two-year-old adopted son Nicholas.

Last night, as the five children —all boys—were recovering in St. Charles's Hospital, Ladbroke Grove, Spike, said: "In giving up his life he left his wife and family unsupported, uninsured, and alone."

Mr. Ayres was in his home in Bevington Road, Notting Hill, on Thursday evening.

Screams

The five children, aged from six years to five months, were in a first-floor room when fire broke out. Mr. Ayres heard the screams, leapt a wall and dashed into the house.

But his attempt was in vain. Spike was told of Mr. Ayres's action by local councillor Mr. Charles Hopkins, who said: "I asked Spike if he would visit Mr. Ayres in hospital, and he agreed right away."

Added Spike, who himself has four children: "I felt so helpless at the hospital. And when I learned that he had died I felt something should be done. Anyone who wishes to help can get in touch with me personally at 9, Orme Court, Bayswater, London."

Derek Marks (Editor)
Daily Express,

25 June 1969

Dear Mr Marks,

Through the columns of your paper, may I thank you for
affording me the opportunity to appeal for funds for Ted Ayres,
(The dustman who died in a fire trying to save children), because
as a result of this within four days of the appeal in your paper, we
received over £1,000.

Once again may I thank you, and all those people who helped
financially.

Yours sincerely,
Spike Milligan

———◆———

Notting Hill
London W10

Dear Mr Milligan,

I would like to thank you so very very much for the kindness and
understanding you have shown to me after the loss of my dear
husband. I cannot find enough words to say how grateful I am to
you and all the wonderful people who have donated to your
appeal. I only wish it were possible to thank each one of them for
their kindness, but most of all my thanks go to you for everything
you have done to make things easier for me and my little boy.

I am,

Your sincerely,
Barbara Ayres

———◆———

Sir Bernard Miles
Mermaid Theatre
London EC4

29 September 1969

Dear Bernard,

Thank you for the tickets for Richard II and thank you for the dinner; but I can't say that of that very up-tight woman who sat between you and I. She needed her arse kicking for a good six months.

But, everything else was fine.

Regards and Love,
Spike Milligan

Sir Bernard Miles
The Mermaid Theatre
London EC4

14 April 1970

Dear Bernard,

Thank you for yours of the 16th along with the article on mutations.

Like you, I get a great overburdening weight of frustration at the way, rather a direction, that man is going. The scientists seem to think that they are going to solve all the problems, and brother, don't we know they are wrong? It would appear that rather than think in terms of birth control to reduce malnutrition, they have assumed the belief that one day they can turn mountains into protein and serve portions of mountains to the starving world.

And then there is, and this is most important, a limit to the number of scientific computations possible on this planet, in other words, there is a limit to the world's commodities because one cannot manufacture anything from nothing; the basis of all scientific experiments is material.

Anyhow, there is a general shift of emphasis made possible by the ordinary man in the street (and brother this means you and I), starting to disagree with people like the Ministry of Agriculture who would go blindly on spraying crops with poisonous chemicals and not stop to investigate the possibility of poison in them. It is small societies such as Soil who have put pressure on the big boys, and has led to the banning of DDT (I am glad to say I am a member of Soil).

So, Bernard, there are small victories starting to come. So keep fighting.

Love, Light and Peace,
Spike Milligan

——•——

Sir Bernard Miles
Mermaid Theatre
London EC4

22 June 1970

Dear Bernard,

Lying in bed on Saturday night I decided that I would drop you a line saying how much I appreciate your image in the world of the theatre. You have done immense good in the face of competition from the big West End theatres, and you have survived. This is no mean feat.

I realise that Lady Miles also played a big part in this and she too I hold in great regard.

Apart from this your attitude as a human being is one of great feeling for fellow men (though the bastards don't deserve it.)

Well that's that off my chest.

Love, light and peace,
Spike Milligan

51%
49%

WILLIAM HOLDEN
CARL HIRSCHMANN

P.O. BOX 35
NANYUKI, KENYA, EAST AFRICA
PHONE NANYUKI 55
CABLE:- SAFCLUB, NANYUKI

MOUNT
KENYA
Safari Club

KENYA   EAST AFRICA

EUROPEAN ADDRESS:
82 TALSTRASSE
ZURICH, SWITZERLAND
PHONE: 051-23 06 21

21 March '70

Dear Norma Life of my life,
      This place, as far as peace and quite,
scenery and luxury, are concerned is the
place for a holiday. We have a private
cottage. Glass wall along the front, which
leads to a sweeping lawn - ~~down to~~ with
peacocks (among them a pure white one),
onto an artifical wild bird pond/lake,
then beyond that the foothills - and finally,
like a well placed centre piece, Mount Kenya -
17,000 feet - snow topped, and an ~~used~~ unending
series of cloud changes about its peak. Stone
fire places with logs crackling into flame pictures,
during the evenings. The bath room has a
sunken bath with room for 4 people
inside. There is nothing to do, except

Walks, swimpool, horse riding, — no radio-
TV, or newspaper, I just swim - and read,
I'm ploughing thru' The White Nile' by
Alan Moorehead, what a splendid writer he
is. The pace never slackens. In an hours time
we fly by 4 Seater plane to Samburu –
a Lodge - completely isolated, by a river - on
a plateau 6 000 feet up. Love to all –
from
Spike

[What happened? The lovely Mr Milligan treating me as a human being.
Where's the monster?]

Punch
London EC4

8 October 1973

Dear Spike Milligan,

I've just been rereading 'Puckoon' yet again, and I wanted to rush
out and tell someone that it really is one of the great comic novels
of all time. Why waste a comment like that on someone who

hasn't written the book? So now I've rushed out and told you. Every time I think of that book, I fall about with respect and envy.

Yours sincerely,
Miles Kington

M. Kington Esq.
Punch

31 October 1973

Dear Miles,

I never dreamed that one day while sitting in a bungalow in Cyprus I would receive a letter from Punch congratulating me on a book I had written. Thank you.

I will be in Australia next January, perhaps you would like to write to me there about 'Adolf Hitler – My Part in his Downfall'.

Love, Light and Peace,
Spike Milligan
Dictated over the 'phone from Cyprus

[A German soldier wrote to Spike for information. They formed a friendship which lasted for years.]

Hans Teske Esq.
Milton Keynes

21 July 1975

Dear Hans,

Apologies for the delay in replying I have been away on tour. Actually I was delighted to get your letter, although as a result of the war – I went in a fit man and came out a neurotic.

However, I'm a Christian, and would like to go on being one. Therefore, what can I do to help. If you ask me specific questions I will try and answer them.

The information you have given me is that you were from January/March near Bou Arada. I was an OB Post Signaller in those days so I was with the Infantry most of the time. Can you tell me what Divisions you were in during that time? Or what Battle Group you were in, were you the Korps Gruppe Webber.

Will you let me know and maybe we can meet in London and we can have a talk.

On the 1st November, 1975 my battery have a re-union at the Printers Devil in London, starting at 6-30p.m. would you like to be our Guest. It's nothing special, just eating, drinking and talking. Do let me know.

Sincerely,
Spike Milligan
Dictated by Spike Milligan and signed in his absence.

Mr Terry Georgas
Pendle Hill High School
Wentworthville
New South Wales
Australia

14 July 1976

Dear Terry,

Time is so brief. I cannot fulfil the complete request, but I will do it in brevitas.

OUTSIDE THE SCHOOL WALLS

Leaving school is the second stage after leaving the womb. In both cases each move introduces a lesser degree of security. There is much more friendship inside school than exists in the outside world of commerce and industry. At school there is no financial gain in doing lessons well, therefore the students are not in financial competition with each other. In the world outside survival depends solely on money. Therefore in that world finance is more important than Christian ethics. Consequently, the standard of relationships is not as human and sincere as one would like, or rather Jesus would like, but if Jesus came again he would not recognise the place.

Therefore when you go forth into this financial amphitheatre you will be conjoined in a much less pleasant world than school and a long way from the security of the womb. However, one can survive at a very cultural level despite the fact that one might not earn as much money as one wished. What I am saying, is that Chopin's Etudes might be enjoyed much more by a poor person than a rich tycoon. There is no saying that a book by T. E. Bates might give greater pleasure to a dustman than Lord Hailsham. The postulation is, we should divide the physical world of money and not let it destroy those sensitivities that appreciate morning rain, trees and all those natural things which come around us with no need to earn a penny.

Therefore, in summarizing, go into the world to earn your bread, but remember that man cannot live by bread alone.

Love, light and peace.

Sincerely,
Spike Milligan

———•———

John Bluthal Esq.
New South Wales
Australia

19 October 1977

Dear John,

Just to thank you very much for looking after my Mother on the trip. I am very grateful to you, and you really are a very fine human being, but just fucking temperamental. Still as you are Jewish you can't have it all ways.

Love from the bionic comic.
Spike Milligan

———•———

Gough Whitlam Esq.
Parliament House
Canberra
Australia

20 December 1977

I am desperately sorry to see you go. It's a small consolation, but it's a human one.

Love, light and peace,
Spike Milligan

Mr & Mrs Eric Worrall
The Australian Reptile Park
New South Wales
Australia

27 November 1978

Dear Eric & Robyn,

I was absolutely stunned and felt very very humble when I got your card saying that you had named a walk-away after me. In life there are some things we would like to be remembered by, and strangely enough there would be three things in my life (1) I would like a mountain named after me or a tree, or a part through a woodland; so your little walk-around in a nature reserve has made my wish come true, so I can cancel the mountain and the tree (I did start building a mountain because no buggar seemed to want to name one after me, so I was doing it myself). I must have left some kind of impression in Woy Woy for such a thing to be bestowed on me.

You might laugh at this, but an Abo Cave across The Rip has also been named Milligan's Cave by an Anthropological Team at Sydney University, when I managed to coax them to go and do an archaeological dig there, during which they turned out quite a few pieces of Abo Artifax. If you want to know what they were, write to John Clegg, at the Sydney University.

Anyhow, you and your work are often in my thoughts, as all other lone rebels who fight the cause of conservation around the world, which as you know is very critical. I hope to be over in Australia soon, and of course, I would love to have one of those Woy Woy dinners with you, and Tass Drysdale, and other people who I like.

I am not sending a Christmas Card, this letter will be in lieu of it, anyhow, Merry Christmas to you sweltering in the Bush, while I am out here scraping the frost off my knickers.

Love, light and peace,
Spike Milligan

———◆———

Lord Miles
Mermaid Theatre
London EC4

4 November 1980

Dear Bernard,

I am dictating this over the telephone, hence the typing. How generous of you to send Shelagh and myself such a lovely present.

I do treasure your friendship, and I don't think I have said that to more than half a dozen people in my life. I saw the mention of your old house in St Johns Wood going up for sale again. I remember those distant days you were among the few people who recognised the talent of Peter Sellers, and may I say myself, and you invited us to dinner at your place. I will never forget that evening it was almost like a painting by Rembrandt, I remember too the farm implements on the wall, and I remember we had red wine, and that was enough for us all.

Love, light and peace,
Spike Milligan

P. S. I already love James Cameron, the last time I saw him we had dinner together in Nairobi, he is a great horizon of a man, dotted with limitless interesting objects.

P. P. S. Did you know that DOG can be spelt C-A-T, but it's pronounced CAT.

[One of Spike's dearest friends. They exchanged lunatic letters. All their lives. One of their daughters was getting married.]

Mr & Mrs Lawrence Drizen
London W1

16 February 1983

Dear Lawrence and Esther,

ROMAN CATHOLIC WEDDINGS

(a) Inclusive of Church, Priest, and two bags
    of rice .... £38.50.
(b) Priest with assistant, and one extra bag
    of rice .... £40.00.
(c) Catholic Priest, with Jewish accent, assistant
    and four bags of rice .... £50.00.
(d) Roman Catholic Shidduch, purple silk to cover
    Roman Catholic Statue (£1. extra), records
    of Frankie Vaughan singing Have Nagilah ...... £3.10.
(e) Frankie Vaughan Live .... £10.00.

Sincerely,
Spike Milligan

Lawrence Drizen Esq.
London W1

10 April 1984

Dear Lawrence,

Things must be desperate when you have to go as far as South Africa to borrow writing paper; you say 'your money is safe' in ENGLAND.

Regarding my daughter's wedding in the local Synagogue, news is they are going to pull it down 'Woodside Park', and me, your local Goy is trying to save it.

The reason for its possible demolition is shortage of Jewish attendances, at the moment we are trying to keep it going by smuggling in Irish Catholics, disguised as Jews, send help – just one genuine Jew might turn the balance.

Anyhow thanks for sending the money, it's about to go on (a) my daughter's wedding, (b) my daughter's wedding, and (c) my daughter's wedding. If only you had had a son, this would never have happened.

Love, light and peace to you all,
Spike Milligan

[This is true. He did try to save Woodside Park Synagogue.]

———◆———

[Lawrence Drizen had asked Spike for a donation to support Israel in the Six-Day War. He donated, but on the condition the money went to healing the wounded.]

Nice letters folks

21 AYMER PARADE.
LONDON. N.2
7ᵗʰ JUNE 1967.

Dear Spike,

It is at times like these when people of all walks of life congregate to help each other. It is ironical that this should be so, but human nature is very peculiar.

Your gift was used towards the purchase of an ambulance and Medical supplies and although the people of Israel cannot thank you themselves, Please accept my thanks on their behalf.

SHALOM

Lawrence

Terence Sheehy Esq.
The Catholic Herald

13 October 1986

Dear Terence,

Oh Jeezus, how nice to get a letter from yez.

Yes, I was always very moved by the story of the St Mary's Juggler; at midnight he came to the altar and did what he could do best, he juggled and did his balancing act before a statue of Our Lady as his tribute. I thought that was so lovely, mind you I think I am lovely and I'm currently entering for The Alternative to Miss World Competition, wearing a National Health Service Truss and holding a red jelly – I mean you never know.

Love, light and peace,
Spike Milligan

———•———

Jimmy Laurie
international comedian/entertainer
New South Wales
Australia

Dear Spike Milligan,

As a long time devoted fan, I would just like to say how much I have enjoyed your books, and of course television series over the years, needless to say the Goon Shows, which ABC Radio are still broadcasting.

Would it be possible to have an autograph? my son loves all your stuff, and spreads the word around Sydney University where he studies law, his name is Craig, he buys all your books (and me being Scottish, borrows them).

You mention a Bill Hall a lot in your book, I remember a very good act which toured the halls when variety was at its height, they were called Hall Norman and Ladd, a musical act, would he the same Hall?

If you could send an autograph I would be very grateful, the headed paper is a misnomer, I am only a humble comic working the clubs etc. in Sydney (and sometimes Woy Woy).

Best wishes for now.

Yours sincerely,
Jimmy Laurie

———◆———

Jimmy Laurie Esq.
New South Wales
Australia

10 March 1988

Dear Jimmy,

Thanks for your letter, yes, Hall Norman and Ladd were the names of the Trio, when I was originally with them playing the guitar it was called the Bill Hall Trio. It started in a barrack room at an organisation called the Central Pool of Artists. A place where soldiers who had been wounded in action and down graded, and who could play an instrument, i.e. the piano etc. were grouped together to entertain the troops. One night one of the acts on the variety bill dropped out and we were asked could we play some music in that spot, which we did, very much in the style of the Hot Club de France, and I thought we could be more spectacular if we came on to the stage in rags, looking as if we were untalented, and this we did, and we became an overnight sensation with the troops in Italy. We continued after the war, and we toured Italy as civilians and then toured around England, but we didn't seem to be getting anywhere, so I dropped out, because I wanted to start writing scripts, and the rest is history. Thank you for writing.

Warm regards,
Spike Milligan

[The beginning of it all with the Bill Hall Trio.]

———◆———

Bill Clark Esq.
Gosford City Orchestra
New South Wales
Australia

14 March 1988

My dear Bill,

What a singular honour for the lad from Woy Woy. I have to say 'yes' because it is indeed a delightful surprise. I really am, for once, lost for words, so yes, yes, yes, yes.

Would you give my love to all the members of the Orchestra from an old time jazz trumpet player.

With a bit of luck I might be out there in Australia for the concert. I have to say I have no idea what the arrangements sound like, one can only hope for the best. Again, thank you very much, and remind the members of the Orchestra that a man can't have everything – where would he put it.

Love, light and peace,
Spike Milligan

[The Gosford City Orchestra asked to perform one of Spike's musical scores.]

———◆———

[Children writing Spike funny letters and drawings from their school. He loved them.]

Class 2
Borrow Wood Junior School
Derby

18 May 1988

> Dear, dear Class Two,
> What can I say about all of you
> Very well done
> Yes, each and every one
> Including Mr Allsopp your Master
> Who sounds like a one man disaster
> I want you to put him in a bed
> Then push him gently off Beachy Head
>
> Love,
> Uncle Spike

[Spike read in the newspaper about a girl who lost her sight from picking up dog mess.]

Mr & Mrs Hall
Lancashire

12 August 1988

Dear Mr & Mrs Hall,

This is for Rachel, I was just horrified about what happened to her.

Tell me, I was thinking would a simple tape recorder, with cassettes, be of any help to her. She could record messages and play songs or poetry, and she could then play any cassettes that

she wanted to buy. As I say, do you think it would be of any help?
Do let me know.

Warm regards,
Spike Milligan

30/8/1988

DEAR SPIKE.

THANK You very much for the beautiful Flowers
Your letter AND the money. It was very kind of you.
The flowers smelt lovely, They were Pink roses
and Freesia. I will probably buy a tape
with the money. Have any of your children's STORIES
books been put on tapes, if so could you please
let me know. I would like to hear your VOICE. if you come
to Blackpool anytime please let us know as I would
like to meet you

Dear Phantom of the Office —
Have S? do let me
know.

LoTS of love

From RACHEL x x x x x x x x x x

x x x x x x x x x x x x x x x x x x x x. x

Penguin Books Ltd
27 Wrights Lane
London W8 5TZ

3 September 1987

Dear Spike,

I am not really writing to you as your editor at Penguin in this instance, but as a fan and a grateful giver of your books to my father. He is just coming through five months of particularly unpleasant illnesses. I just wanted to say how utterly grateful I am for the existence of the Military Memoirs, as they have lightened a very, very difficult time for my father. He is enjoying every one of them and is hungry for the next. At the moment we are up to no. 6, which I am holding back to heighten his sense of expectation. I really cannot impress upon you enough how thrilled I have been to have these books to entertain him in a very, very difficult period.

With grateful thanks.

Yours sincerely,
Geraldine Cooke

Ms Geraldine Cooke
Penguin Books Limited
London W8

11 September 1987

Dear Geraldine,

Thank you for what I thought a delicious letter, it was like the morning dew on the grass. It was read over the 'phone to me by my Manager Norma (who is a very fine reader of letters – especially mine) and after hearing the contents it made me feel ever so humble. I thought it is quite amazing when one man's recollections of the humorous side of the war could give pleasure to another man, who he has never met, through the interception of his daughter somehow made life worth living for the next 24 hours. After that of course, next is the rates bill.

Warm regards,
Spike Milligan

———◆———

Sean Milligan Esq
Worcestershire

5 December 1989

My dear son Sean,

Here is a gift for Christmas so you might like to buy whatever you really want. You don't have to pay tax on this as it is a gift.

 If you have any queries phone Norma who sitteth on the right hand of God the Father Almighty.

Your ever loving Dad,
Signed in his absence
primarily because he was not there

———◆———

Dr Alan Borg
Imperial War Museum
London SE1

26 February 1990

Dear Alan Borg,

Your letter 22nd February to hand. I don't think you have got the message. When I pick up a phone I don't pick up to hear a snatch of music, neither the beginning nor the end; it might appeal to idiots to get a piece of music which fortuitously plays one or two or three bars depending how long you are kept hanging on. If people like this they must be music paraplegics; if I want to hear good music I go to the Albert Hall. At the same time this music is eating up the world's energy.

I will repeat again I cannot see anyone but the most asinine creature listening to a few stray bars here and there. It is like buying a book and reading the centre three pages. Either you wipe it off or I will not be a patron.

Unfortunately you are probably one of these high tech individuals who believe people will listen to bits of music and accept it as the right thing. Believe me, as a musician it should not be allowed and I can only repeat, it is not good music.

Sincerely,
Spike Milligan

Field Marshal Bramall KG, GCB, OBE, MC, JP
c/o The Imperial War Museum
London SE1

20 August 1990

Dear Field Marshal Bramall,

I write as a long standing friend of the Imperial War Museum and in my time I have given and traced many valuable photographs and I still continue to do so, until somebody thought it was clever to put this 'Hold' music on the telephone. I find it an insult to the composer and an insult to my intelligence to have to listen to three bars of Brahms and then to be cut off and put through on the line. They are not playing the whole tune it is very aggravating and a waste of money. I wrote to Doctor Alan Borg and complained about it and he seemed to be quite indifferent. I would like to know exactly whose idea it was. You do realise nobody ever hears one of these pieces of music in its entirety it is all chopped up like sausage. All the musicians like myself find it odious, stupid and unnecessary, and I would ask you to ask the Trustees to consider removing this music. If so I would be willing to go on being a friend to the Imperial War Museum otherwise you are losing a very valuable donor.

Sincerely,
Spike Milligan

Imperial War Museum
London SE1 6HZ

24 August 1990

Dear Mr Milligan,

Thank you very much for your letter of 20 August about the recorded music on the Imperial War Museum's telephone line. I am bound to say I find it pretty irritating, too, and I have asked the staff to consider alternative ways of indicating to callers that they are still connected. In the meantime, the existing music has been switched off.

I am grateful to you for taking the trouble to write to me. We do enormously appreciate your support for the Museum's activities and your generous donations to its collections. I do hope you will feel able to continue as a friend and I hope we may have the opportunity of meeting at one of the Museum's future functions.

Yours sincerely,
Edwin Bramall

———◆———

Field Marshal The Lord Bramall KG, GCB, OBE, MC, JP
Imperial War Museum
London SE1

28 August 1990

My dear Field Marshal Lord Bramall,

I cannot believe that there is somebody in the World who can actually do something positive to benefit our social circumstances. I cannot believe that you have managed to switch off that appalling music I can only thank you on behalf of all those who abhor this intrusion and insult to music. I might point out that in the new public toilets at Shepherds Bush they have music which comes on as you enter, music to defecate to must be the final insult to the composer.

My very warm thanks,
Spike Milligan
Ex Lance Bombardier RA
(4th Generation Gunners)

[Such a heartfelt telegram from Peter it haunts me. It didn't happen. He died two months later. 'As we were' could never be. That is what is so chilling. It was a reminder of his deep unhappiness.]

16ᵗʰ June 1992.

Dear Spike,

At long bloody last
they have done something, and
a CBE is nice to have, although
I think they should have at
least made you a Silver Stick to
the Queen, or the Marquis of Granby
or something.

What really matters is
that the great British public —
including me — think you are
the greatest, and no honour is
really going to do justice to your
marvellous original talent.

Love always,

George ____..

[From George Martin.]

George Martin Esq
Wiltshire

11 August 1992

My dear George

Thank you for your letter, I searched the envelope desperately but there was no money in it.

Thank you for all you say, it actually wasn't the British public that got me this award, it was a solicitor who wrote to the 'Awards Department' pointing out that I should get one, without him it would not exist – so there you are.

Lots of love,
Spike

P. S. Remember if ever you want a good lyricist, he is now a CBE.

TELEMESSAGE

Carpenters Meadows
Dumb Womans Lane
Udimore Rye Sussex
TN31 6AD

08 February 1993

TELEMESSAGE LXP   ROSES
NORMA FARNES
9 ORM COURT
BAYSWATER
LONDON W2 4RI.

I HAVE TO PHONE YOU EVERY DAY LIKE WATER TO THE FLOWER LIKE HONEY TO
THE BEE, YOU SUSTAIN ME.

LOVE SPIKE

*[What the hell had he done, or wanted me to do, that he knew I wouldn't
want to do?]*

Index

Page references in **bold** indicate facsimile copies.